FROM NEW LINE MANAGER TO GREAT PEOPLE LEADER

(or What Henry the Hoover can teach you about people leadership)

TABLE OF CONTENTS

Dedications/Thankyous

Firstly, I'd like to thank my fantastic wife, Melissa for her support and encouragement whilst I've done this, and for helping me with the proof reading and to my two stepsons Andy and Seb who both motivate and inspire me in more ways than they could ever realise. It was Seb's book "Social Marketing Success" which gave me the toolkit to realise how I could start to take my sideline and grow it into a full time job by using social media.

In addition, I would like to thank Sam Eaton from Mindability Consulting who Melissa introduced me to and who recognised that I had it in me to run my own business and gave me the support and encouragement to get there, even on the days when nothing was working and I was getting frustrated. If you want a good business coach and you're in the HR profession, look no further than Sam!

CHAPTER 1

INTRODUCTION

Why write a book aimed at first time line managers?

Chances are, if you've picked up this book you've just been promoted to being a line manager – or people leader as I prefer to call you, or you could be a business owner about to take on their first employees as you're growing.

Don't get me wrong, being a people leader can be a wonderful and vastly rewarding thing.

- You get to impart your knowledge and wisdom on other people

- You can help people grow and develop in their careers and you can see them going on to achieve bigger and better things because you've enabled them to have that development

- You can also learn new skills yourself about how the human mind works and apply those techniques to get the best out of your team.

- You don't need to be loud and outgoing to be a successful people leader either – different personality types can work equally well in the role.

However, quite often being a positive people leader does have challenges and that's what my book aims to help you with. As one of my wiser LinkedIn contacts said to me, "every problem in a business is a leadership problem." Which means that as Leaders you need to be clued up on how to resolve it.

Does any of the following resonate with you?

- You lack confidence in what you can and can't say to your team, and are worried you may say the wrong thing, or someone will take out a grievance against you?

- You feel imposter syndrome because you've never managed anyone else before and think that someone will "find you out".

- You have a absence/grievance/disciplinary case up and coming

- You don't know how to "step up" and manage your former colleagues if you've been promoted internally.

- You don't have the confidence to have a difficult conversation.

- You don't know how to guide a team through change

- Your team is made up of different people with different personalities and differing needs

- You feel like your employee's personal counsellor

- You're scared to ask your manager for help because they hired/promoted you into this position.

If so, don't worry, I can help you. Because I've been there myself and I understand the pain points and can help you overcome these.

Every year lots of people get promoted into their first people leadership position. And they've usually got there because they're technically good at what they do in the day job. But it doesn't mean that they'll automatically be a good people leader. Sadly, many companies don't always provide any real training or support to help someone develop the skills that are needed to step up and manage a team. For me, putting someone on a one to two day "Management Course" doesn't mean they will come out of the classroom a fully fledged people leader. Chances are, they'll think it was interesting but put the notes in their bottom drawer and leave them to gather dust whilst they carry on trying to manage their team.

Grievances raised and employment tribunal claims often are the result of poor leadership, and/or an inexperienced manager not understanding the red flags and stopping a situation getting out of control. According to Gov.uk, 18,000 tribunal claims were made in the UK between January-March 2022. That's a lot of time and money companies will have to spend defending those.

I know when I took on my first line manager role some 20 years ago I absolutely sucked at it! I had no training, advice, mentoring, support or anything that would help me succeed in it. But I used that experience to learn, go onto become a successful people leader and to spend my career advising and supporting a wide variety of managers from first line supervisors, to Managing Directors, Business Owners and CEO's on how to get the best out of their people. Whilst I hated it at the time, that was probably one of the best things that could have happened to me early on in my career as it meant I learned more from my mistakes than if it had all run smoothly, and I wouldn't have had the experience to draw on that helped me become a better HR person and a better people leader.

It still astounds me that so many companies still take a very unstructured, haphazard approach to this, or just expect people to be able to step up and become great leaders because they are great Sales People, Accountants, Engineers, IT Technicians etc. This worries me because if people are not managed correctly or well, they'll start to feel unmotivated, frustrated and more likely to leave an organisation leading to higher turnover and therefore higher replacement costs as well as a feeling of uncertainty and demotivation for those left behind.

Either way, it doesn't make for a great culture or that team/organisation being a great place to work. We live in a world where employees can write negative reviews on sites like Glassdoor or Indeed which highlight exactly these types of issues in a very public way.

However, there is a solution to all this, and it's not about sending people on a short training course on how to be a manager and expecting them to come out of the classroom as ready made people managers. It's about helping those individuals have the right approaches from the start in easy, bite sized stages and developing the right people skills so they feel confident to deal with any situation they may encounter from their team, and/or, their own manager.

This is where having a people expert like myself coaching your people leaders in how to deal with people situations can really save a lot of time, stress and costs as I help leaders identify those red flags and help them prevent, rather than cure a situation.

There's lots of books out there on how to manage and lots of management theories. I've tried to deliberately steer clear of these theories and instead write this book based on some sensible, practical advice based on my own experiences and that of other people who've kindly allowed me to use their stories in this book.

So this is the book that I wish I'd had when I took on my first line management role in my 20's, although many parts of it are relevant to people leaders at any stage in their careers.

I'll also give you easy tips to support you after reading this book so you have the confidence to deal with the types of situations you may encounter. Whilst there's not a text book answer for everything, you will find the same kind of situations can keep cropping up again and again and you can adapt how you deal with them depending on the individual(s) in question.

Doug Betts

Ipswich, UK, May 2023.

CHAPTER 2

WHO AM I AND WHAT CAN YOU LEARN FROM ME?

Why did I leave a well paid HR role and prefer instead to go fully self employed as an Independent HR Consultant and Coach? For me, it was because it's good to take a calculated risk from time to time and it's something I'd been thinking of doing for many years but the 2020 pandemic finally inspired me to try and turn my "side hustle" into a full time role.

I do this because I want to make a difference to the world of work by helping business owners to create great workplaces with a great culture and great people in them – leading to less turnover, less time spent re-recruiting, less staffing issues and therefore more profit and enabling the business to spend more time doing what it was designed to do in the first place.

In turn, this makes people managers far less stressed, more productive, and happier in their roles as they have the confidence to tackle people issues and to get the best out of their teams.

I get massive job satisfaction from helping people, and see-ing workplaces get better because of something I've recommended introducing, whether that's a new culture, a new way of working, or because I've coached a nervous new people leader and gone onto see them excel at managing their team and grow in confidence.

I was inspired to write this book because whilst there are many independent HR Consultants and Coaches out there who will offer advice or off the shelf products I wanted to give something more bespoke and use my 20+ years as an HR professional in a different way. Having worked up to Director level in "in house" roles I want to put my knowledge and experience out there to help you as line managers become confident in how to manage your people.

I still get frustrated about people's misconceptions about what an HR professional should do. If you hire an Accountant or an IT Support Person it's usually quite clear to the manager/business owner what the expectations are, but for HR, it's a more blurred line. Over the years, my experience has meant that I am able to get involved with all of the following to support my clients:-

- Reporting and data analytics

- Compliance Checks e.g. contracts of employment, handbook, setting up processes for running a successful HR function.

- Working with Senior Leadership Teams to establish a Company's Values, Culture and embed it across all practices in the organisation.

- Designing and Implementing a People Strategy/Plan that's aligned with the Company's vision, mission and goals.

- Undertaking job evaluation and comparing pay and benefits to similar organisations so companies remain competitive

- Designing and Delivering Training and Coaching Programmes taking people from functional managers to great people leaders.

- Monitoring sickness absence and advising managers on how to get people back to work

- Recruiting new hires.

- Coaching Mangers through Investigations, Disciplinaries, Grievances, Capability procedures (which should only be used as a last resort – a manager and employee talking early on is much more effective!)

- Preparing cases for an employment tribunal

- Organisational Design, Restructuring and Redundancies.

- Consultations to go through mergers/acquisitions as well as changing terms and conditions.

- Implementing HR information systems

More bizarrely, I have also found myself responsible for taking photos of all new hires for their ID cards in my first ever role – odd what HR people are sometimes asked to do! Don't get me started on my views about whether HR should be organising the Christmas Party!.....

My Values

When I started looking at my business I thought about who I'd looked up to and admired and respected in the past. I realised that all my real life and fictional heroes and heroines had one thing in common – they were positive disruptors. That is, they didn't accept conventional wisdom and went about doing things their own way, whilst changing their environment for the better.

Here's my values:-

Value	Brief Meaning
Continuous Improver	I seek to continually learn and improve my knowledge. I learn from my mistakes and practice humility. I will believe in myself but be open to constructive criticism
Positive Disruptor	I will always ask "why" and question things I won't be afraid to have difficult conversations when needed. I will constructively challenge others and myself.
Purposeful Achiever	I use my time wisely to get results. I am ambitious and want to make a positive difference in what I do. I will be decisive and not f*** about unnecessarily.
Diversity Celebrant	I celebrate and respect people who are different to me. I will always look to find common ground and connection.
Real Human	I will be my authentic self and march to my own beat. I will do the right thing even when no one's looking. I will be there for people when they need me.

Why HR and why would you want to learn from an HR professional?

When I was at School I always wanted to become a Teacher. Looking back I can't remember why other than I guess it was a job I was watching people do on a daily basis, some better than others! Much as I enjoyed it, a week of work experience at my old primary school whilst in Year 10 made me think better of it. However, the desire to learn and help others never went away.

I went into my first office job aged 22, working for a local accident management insurance company. I spent the first two weeks of employment with my fellow new hires on a very comprehensive training programme about how to use the company's software, and how to process claims. At the end of the two weeks, I was told to "forget all that – you're going to be dealing with cars that have been declared insurance write offs". So I was then thrown into the deep end and left to figure things out through trial and error, with a less than helpful "buddy".

I knew after two days that this wasn't the right job for me and I did everything I could to find something else that I'd enjoy more. I got into HR (Human Resources) or "Personnel" as it was still called back then in some places, because I wanted to help people learn in the workplace. I have a logical brain so for me I wanted someone in my insurance job to talk me through the process from start to finish, to explain not just what to do but why and also any potential pitfalls to watch out for, or mistakes others had made I could learn from. I wanted people to have a better learning experience at work than I'd just had.

So whilst I got into HR to develop adults in the Workplace, and I have done that, I got happily distracted by many of the other things an HR Department gets involved with. I developed a particular interest in Employment Law, Change Management and Benefits/Pay analysis.

I'd wanted to have my own HR Consultancy for some time. It began almost by accident when a few local business owners I knew approached me and asked for help, usually to sort out a tricky employee situation or write contracts/policies. The work was few and far between as I still had a full-time day job. They didn't need and couldn't afford a full time HR person but wanted someone they trusted who would give them advice around their people. I had previously worked full time for an already established HR Consultancy so that gave me an idea of the kind of work that would be done and the structure.

During the pandemic I, like many other people had a rethink about what I wanted out of life and my career. I was inspired by several people I have known who had started their own ventures. From a personal perspective I knew what I was taking on would be difficult, different to the "day job" and would involve me learning a whole new set of skills, but I was up for the challenge. I also realised I didn't want to commute to the same office every day any more, and wanted to work where and when I wanted to without having to ask permission for annual leave. That said, I knew the reality would be I would be working more than my job's contracted hours to be able to get this business off the ground.

Like many other small businesses, it took me a while to get established and to find new clients but slowly and surely they came, and I have been lucky enough to work for some great companies and meet some brilliant business owners and teams, as well as some that needed my help to turn themselves around.

I've been fully self employed since the start of 2023 and was very grateful to my last employer for helping me transition from full time, to part time, to fully self employed so it didn't feel like the cliff edge that many solopreneurs are faced with. I still have lots I want to achieve with my business and look forward to continuing to grow it in the coming years and to see just how far I can go.

My Company's called Sure Betts HR Solutions Ltd. Why did I choose that name? Apart from the pun using my surname

I think it works well for a people focussed consultancy business because Betts = Gambling.

For me, the analogy is that gambling is only meant for fun, and when the fun stops you need to stop.

Having an employee or yourself who may be unqualified in employment law or interview processes hiring a member of staff can be a gamble and may even be breaking the law.

Firing a member of staff without the correct procedures in place can be a gamble, and could cost you more than what you've paid them.

Not mentoring or having the time for your staff's wellbeing can be a gamble.

Why put things to chance or luck when you know with gambling the house always wins?

You wouldn't gamble with your business finances – you'd hire a qualified accountant, so why gamble with the people in your business by trying to google employment law or downloading old contract and policy templates off the internet?

You need a certainty, you need the right procedures, processes and a modern approach to people management.

Don't leave it to luck. What you need is a Sure Betts Solution.

PART ONE

WHAT DOES GOOD HR SUPPORT AND A GOOD PEOPLE LEADER LOOK LIKE?

CHAPTER 3

WHAT HR IS AND ISN'T, AND HOW IT CAN HELP YOU IN YOUR ROLE AS A PEOPLE MANAGER

As I've mentioned in my introduction, over my career I've worked with many people who have an odd misconception about what a People/HR department should do. If you're reading this you may already have a HR person in place in your business or it could be done by an outsourced company like mine. I am on a mission to get businesses to see HR as an enabler not a blocker, and to move away from the reputation of being the "angel of doom".

The point I want to make here is that a good People function in, or working for your business should be doing things like this:-

- The Head of the Department/HR Consultant has a direct reporting line to the MD/Board/CEO/Other Directors so they can advise on the Company's business plans/strategy from a People perspective. All too often I've seen HR as being the last people to find out about key things which they should know about from an early stage such as change of shareholders, sale of Company, mergers and acquisitions, planned growth, planned restructuring or redundancies, loss of revenue/profit.

- Get to know you, your business, what you do, what its culture is, and how it ticks so they can give you the best advice when it comes to managing your people.

- Help managers get the right skills to attract and hire the best talent. The manager who thinks recruitment is just about picking the one you like the best will not last long in a world where things are constantly being disrupted, and there's a need to keep up to date with the latest thinking around how to hire the best candidates. Doing what worked 5, 10 + years ago won't necessarily work now. The best candidates don't hang around for weeks waiting for you to review their CV, as the chances are they will have lots of applications on the go so you need to move fast, but beware of things like unconscious bias, and asking the right interview questions/using the right selection methods to avoid a costly mis-hire. All things a good People expert can help you do. Also avoid waiting for "the perfect candidate" e.g. the golden flying unicorn that doesn't exist.

- Helping create good positive experiences for employees whilst they are at work. This involves advising on, helping to create, but not leading on Culture (everyone should play a part in this), and advising on how a Company can best engage and motivate their employees, in the hope that they may then hang around a bit longer, remain loyal to you and cost less in turnover/loss of talent.

- Helping an organisation look after its employees and do the right thing by them – this could be including wellbeing initiatives (but not in a parental, "we know what's best for you" way; and also helping to create career pathways for people who want to progress within a Company.

- Helping a workforce to develop the right skills needed to be future proof.

- Use the right technology to find out insights and data about the workforce which can be used for future planning.

- Comparing your pay and benefits to the market to make sure they remain competitive.

- Making sure that the legal HR processes are in place but are not overly burdensome.

- Advising on change processes to help a business or individuals within it move from position A to position B whilst remaining legally compliant.

- Helping to exit people from an organisation when their time is up, but in a dignified way.

- **Be on hand to give coaching and advice to managers on how to deal with their people, and acting as a sounding board as it's ok as a manager to not always know the answer to something but know you need to ask a professional expert before acting.**

In short, being a trusted people expert who knows how to add value, knows employment law, knows how to get the best out of people and knows how to stop difficult situations escalating.

This is why, in my opinion, you shouldn't just have the People function in your business overseen by your Accountant, PA, or Finance Director! It's taken me 20+ years to learn my craft and do it well. You shouldn't trust a non qualified person to undertake an HR function any more than you'd ask me, or any other HR professional to file your annual Company Accounts for you.

I would also say that you should not engage with me to work with you if you expect me to do anything on the following list, because it's not what a people function should do and it won't get the best value out of my knowledge and experience.

- Organising the staff Christmas party/Annual Conference/ Be the Purveyor of enforced jollity. It may be loosely termed as "wellbeing" or "engagement" but best left to a professional who has events planning in their skills set.

- Admin. OK, every job involves some element of this even at Director level but what a good HR person shouldn't be doing is nothing but admin, pushing bits of paper between pillar and post just for the sake of it. (processing absence forms for example, when a good system can automate this, even if you're a small business)

- Managing someone's employees when things get a little difficult. HR are not the thought police (to take on that parental role of reminding everyone to behave at the Xmas party or when it's too snowy for the workplace to remain open). Nor are HR the fashion police (to enforce a dress code). A good HR person can sit with you, advise you on what to say, on the process but no way should they be doing it on your behalf. You're the people leader, that's your job! The aim of this book is to help you feel more confident in having these types of conversations and making those decisions.

- Processing/Managing people's holiday requests. Get a decent system to do that for you, or if you have a limited budget and only a few employees, use a spreadsheet.

- Decide who should be hired/fired or made redundant. We may have to help you carry that out, but the decision is yours as the manager.

- Health and Safety/Facilities/Data Protection etc. They're specialisms in their own right and shouldn't really be undertaken by an HR Person unless they also hold a professional qualification in those areas.

Interlude: What Henry the Hoover can teach you about people leadership

When I took on my first HR Advisor level role in my late 20's it was at a large public sector organisation where there was every type of case and employee issue possible that came through the team. Our job was to support Managers with a variety of (or lack of) skills around each one. This was definitely a sink or swim job for me that would either give me the confidence to carry on in the HR profession or crawl back under a stone. Thankfully, it was the latter. Whilst we had every type of issue this role also taught me the "gold standard" for dealing with these things (it was also the workplace where I met my future wife!)

So where does Henry the Hoover fit into all of this? My first ever case, as a nervous newly promoted HR Advisor was to deal with an "incident" where an employee had been found in a store cupboard in a compromising position with part of Henry the Hoover wrapped around one of their private parts. I admit that one of the biggest challenges was to try and get through the advice calls without laughing. Thankfully or sadly, depending on how you look at it the individual in question resigned before the disciplinary took place. So what lessons can be drawn from this particular tale?

- People Leaders should expect the unexpected. If they can deal with this they can deal with anything.

- People Leaders need to try and find out employee's motivation behind their actions, as well as not assume that everyone knows how to behave at work, but also not just hide behind lengthy policies and rules and have difficult conversations

- Being a people leader can suck sometimes (quite literally in this case ☐) but it can also be rewarding and you can grow in confidence dealing with difficult situations.

- You need a sense of humour too and a good sounding board for advice.

CHAPTER 4

MANAGER OR LEADER AND WHAT MAKES A GOOD ONE?

Take a moment to look back on the career you've had to date and think about the best line manager you ever had. Think about how they made you *feel* about your job, your place in the organisation you were working in, and what it was about them that made you want to work for them.

Now think about the worst manager you've ever had and why you didn't want to work for them, how they made you feel about your role etc.

Of course there's no such thing as a total villain or a total hero. People Leaders like yourself are human beings too with your own imperfections and insecurities. Hopefully, you will be able to also have seen the weaknesses in your favourite manager as well as find at least one good thing to say about the worst manager. These thoughts will often shape your own thinking about the kind of people manager that you want to be.

There are many theories out there about the different styles of "Management" (as opposed to "Leadership") One of the most well-known identifies 4 styles as being

- Autocratic ("do as you're told")

- Democratic ("I must consult everyone before making a decision)

- Laissez-Faire ("hands off")

- Transformational (developing a vision and encouraging the team to get on board to achieve a goal).

To read further about these styles, take a look at https://www.uagc.edu/blog/4-leadership-styles-in-business. There are times and places when each style is and isn't appropriate to use.

Whilst the terms "Management" and "Leadership" are often used interchangeably, For me, Leadership is more about being able to influence and inspire people to contribute towards the overall success of their team/organisation rather than Management which is more about control. I have tried where possible to refer to the term "People Leader" in this book as that's what I want you, the reader to become.

Here's my summary of the key differences between the two:-

Manager	Leader
Leads tasks/resources through maintaining status quo and compliance with that	Encourages and empowers people to think differently and constructively challenge things
Keen to achieve short term goals	Looks towards achieving/setting long term visions
Focus on work and output	Focus on getting people to buy in and change hearts and minds
Transactional style e.g. focus on process, statistics, logic	Transformational style e.g. focus on change and evolution as the business develops, looks at continuous improvement.
Will have direct reports working for them	People will follow them and be inspired by them even if they don't report directly into them.
Likely to follow rules	Likely to take risks and create new rules
Plans, organises resources	Inspires and motivates people to achieve goals

Chron (Ref: https://smallbusiness.chron.com/top-signs-poor-leadership-31537.html) identifies poor leadership as:-

- Where there's no team chemistry

- There's no communication

- There's high employee turnover

- There's micro management

- There's no vision

- There's no clear expectations of employees

- The Manager has favourites

- The Manager is a bully

- The Manager tolerates poor performance and behaviour leading to others becoming demotivated.

- Where people don't feel that they are serving a useful purpose

- Where people feel excluded from key information/the team

To me a good leader isn't there to "tell people what to do" as that harks back to the command and control style of management which doesn't have much place in the modern workforce unless you're in a high pressure situation such as in the Police, or Fire service. For me, good leadership is a mix of things such as showing integrity, being a visionary thinker and persuading others to come on that journey with you, being able to influence and persuade others, but also knowing when to back down and compromise. It's also about self awareness, listening first and speaking later, praising the team you're leading and showing empathy (not sympathy) towards them.

Tanmay Vora explains how influence is a by-product of your own actions and says

"To me, the ability to influence is an essential leadership skill. To influence is to have an impact on the behaviours, attitudes, opinions and motivation of team members. Influence is not to be confused with power or authority. It's not about manipulation or forcing one's decision on others to get your own way"

In one of his many social media posts, Steven Bartlett of Dragon's Den and Diary of a CEO fame defines these as being the signs of a great company culture:-

- People make friends at work

- People have a high level of trust

- People celebrate each other's wins

- People feel a sense of a team effort

- People feel comfortable to ask for help

- People can express their honest opinion

- People have the room to try new things and be bold

- People feel like they have authority within their role.

Take a moment to think about your team, and your workplace. How many of those things are currently in place? And for the things that aren't what do you as a leader need to do to change the culture to enable those things to happen. For me, if you are a great leader then these statements will be true about your team.

Case Study 1: Thanks to one of my LinkedIn Contacts for allowing me to use their story in my book:

My favourite manager was a self-made woman in many ways. I could tell that she was doubtful about working with me when I first met her and she grilled me a bit about my experience. However, she very rapidly saw that I was eager to learn and that led very quickly to a camaraderie and a friendship over time which I still cherish today. She trusted me with her files when she was unavailable and made sure that I got the credit when she returned.

My worst manager cared only about himself. He was constantly stressed, left me juggling his caseload alongside my own for the best part of a year, making me think that it was all my responsibility before finally stepping in with some "suggestions" that I'd already come up with myself and, when he was around, insisted on discussing clients' matters with me before having a call with the client when he promptly stole my advice and pretended that it was his own right in front of me (luckily, I'm savvy enough to have kept the best bits of advice to provide to the client myself).

Perhaps you have had similar experiences to my connection? The key thing as a new manager is that you learn from the mistakes and successes of managers past and present.

When I did this exercise based on my own experiences this is what I came up with:-

Good People Leaders….	Bad Line Managers…
Gave me interesting problems to solve	Didn't listen to my suggestions or ideas
Trusted me	Had a "my way or the highway" approach
Were there for support and advice when I needed it	
Were open to new ideas	Felt threatened by anyone/thing new
Said thanks for a job well done	Micro Managed
Gave constructive feedback	Gave me a to do list
Gave me more responsibility when they knew I could handle it	Gave me menial repetitive tasks
	Gave feedback once a year
Let me shadow them	Wanted to control everything themselves
Made time to have 1:1 conversations with me	Criticised, never praised
Treated me like an adult	Didn't back me up to other people when I'd done the right thing.
Made me feel….	**Made me feel….**
Empowered	Disengaged
Trusted	"are they out to get me"?
Motivated	Paranoid
Secure as I could trust them	Like just a number on the payroll
More likely to open up to them in an honest way	

I think you can sum up the "bad" manager qualities into four main types:-

- The micromanager. The one who's constantly looking over shoulders, who doesn't trust anyone to do anything without checking with them first.

This type of manager definitely won't cope well with hybrid or remote staff and will actively holding back employees from learning new skills and developing in their roles.

- The dysfunctional manager – this is the manager who isn't actually that good at their job. They lack leadership skills, they are indecisive, they might even be lazy.

Whatever the thing is that's stopping them from excelling, if you're their manager, you need to decide if it's something that can be rectified or not. Often, training and development can work wonders for this kind of manager.

- The bullying manager – this is probably the worst of the bunch. Because if a manager is bullying direct reports, it creates a terrible workplace culture and one that can be very difficult to fix.

It means your people dread coming into work, they're not engaged, and you'll probably find you have an increased staff turnover (and poor company reputation to boot).

- The climber – this kind of manager has only their best interests at the heart of their actions and decisions.

They'll do anything in their power to look good to their superiors, and don't take much interest in their team. They probably also see colleagues as competitors which can create tension and a bad atmosphere.

Any one of these managers has the potential to create a terrible atmosphere in a workplace, to increase absence rates and staff turnover, and to tear a company culture apart.

Of course the above isn't by any means meant to be a scientific exercise. It's meant to stir up emotion about how you felt about good and bad experiences at work. I do this because line management isn't about always having a text book answer to everything, or treating people in the same way. Because we are human beings. We're unique. We think and feel things. We like to feel connected, wanted, like we're making a valuable contribution to the work that we do. And we want a manager who will support us in doing so. So here's the first tip I'll give you.

Tip 1: Don't treat everyone the same, but treat everyone fairly.

A manager sometimes has to deliver the same piece of bad news to two different people. If a manager knows the people in their team well, they will know that they still need to motivate their team and it's how they give that message that is the main issue. Person A may just want to be given the cold, hard facts and be given time to go away and process them and then come back with their thoughts, whereas Person B may need a softer approach, a metaphorical hug, a coffee meeting, and a discussion there and then about how they are feeling about this. A good manager will get to understand how each of their people ticks and adjust their style accordingly depending on who they're talking to.

Managing Upwards

I also want to take a moment to talk about how you manage your own manager. The first thing to remember is that your manager is also a human being and they too have fears, insecurities as well as positive points. You may really look up to them as an inspirational leader, or you may also feel a sense of frustration with them.

Clearly, one piece of advice will not suit all circumstances. The best way to build a relationship with your manager is to ask them up front what their expectations are of you in the role if they've not clearly expressed this already. Also find out what makes them tick, and use that to build a relationship with them. You don't have to like them, but find out how to successfully influence them.

For example, imagine you are asking for money for a project or to take on a new member of staff and your Manager has the final sign off on it. Based on what you know about them what will make them most likely to agree to it – a solid business case backed up with facts and logic, or more of an emotional argument about the pain the business will face if the project/hire doesn't go ahead. You need to adapt your style. Sometimes going as far as making them think your idea is their idea can work.

A lot of my clients tell me they also find it difficult to challenge their manager. A good manager will welcome feedback, but others may feel threatened by it. The best advice I can give here is again, get to know your manager and if you have to say something, say it calmly, politely but firmly and be as constructive as possible.

Conclusions

There's definitely a place in the modern workforce for good Managers as well as good Leaders. There are times when a good leader will adopt a different approach depending on their circumstances. A good example of this is a Chief Inspector of Police I worked with some years ago who was fully qualified to operate a fire arms unit. In those circumstances of a high risk situation she could realise that her leadership style needed to be very "Command and Control", whereas with the project I was working with her on, which was looking at how the HR function should be improved - she needed to be more collaborative.

The key is knowing which style to adopt and when, and if possible combine the best of both.

I think Gerry Robinson, a troubleshooter for the NHS put this very clearly when he said in an interview with the Radio Times

"People think Management is some kind of scientific art form. It's not! Management is about the most basic of things – talk to people, listen to people, find out what needs to be done and do it"

I think that's good advice to remember. That, and don't be a dick....

CHAPTER 5

HUMANS, NOT ASSETS

I have a real dislike of the over used phrase "our people are our greatest asset". It's meant well when Business Leaders say this, and the sentiment is correct in that without people, you don't have a business. People buy from people so it's the personalities, and their skills that will make your business more profitable than your competitors.

However assets to me are fixed things which sit on a Company's balance sheet and depreciate year after year. People don't do that, and they also cannot be treated the same. A good people leader will recognise this and adapt their style depending on the individuals as per the example I gave in the previous chapter.

Tip 2: Always think "Am I treating my team as adults and as humans"

Lucy Adams, the founder of Disruptive HR in her book "HR Disrupted" follows an EACH model where she gives tips for making sure that everything you do is treating your employees as Adults, Consumers and Human Beings.

So when you're taking up your first line management position how can you make sure you have a human centred approach when dealing with your team?

From my own experience – you need get to know them as people – and quickly! Find out what their partners, children, pets are called, what they like to do outside of work, what football team they support (if any), what they like to drink, (if anything). Spend some quality 1:1 time with them, especially in the early days. It really does help to build a rapport and trust. This may sound obvious but if you don't do this, how are they going to connect with you and, more importantly, trust you? They need to relate to you as a person.

Likewise, it's important that you don't appear as an enigma to them either. If you're like me and don't tend to overshare personal information this may be difficult, but my advice is to give something about yourself away to them as well. It doesn't have to be something you'd only want to share with a psychologist! But it helps break down barriers and help them get to know you, like you and trust you. Meaning when things get tough at work they're more likely to approach you for advice which is exactly what you want. If you don't you may be wrongly perceived as a distant and uncaring robot.

You may turn into their unofficial counsellor and confidant which is OK to a point, but you also need to know when to sign post them to someone else if they need more professional help that you can't give (hint: it doesn't mean telling them to "talk to HR" when the going gets tough and you don't want to have a difficult conversation with them"!)

As for treating them like adults, this is about recognising just that. They are adults. They are more likely to respond well if you help them make their own decisions and choices rather than give them endless policies to read and sign to say they've understood, or threaten them with disciplinary action if they fail to do X, Y, and Z. Or giving them an annual appraisal with a score. Or micro managing their every move. Think about how you'd feel if that was/has been/is done to you. Chances are you may feel like you're not trusted and may start to act accordingly, or only go by the rules.

Yes of course it's sensible to have some rules in place, and operate in a legally compliant environment, but too many of these will stifle innovation. And it's innovation that can give organisations that much needed competitive edge.

It's important to remember that you as a manager are a human being too and you need to foster a mentality of "We're all in this together" (Sorry to have to use philosophy from *High School Musical* here but it's true!) You need to always be thinking of others, check in regularly with your team, and remember to offer help even to those who may seem to be coping well. Be flexible and compassionate. We need human-centred leadership. We need leaders with a heart for people.

What isn't needed is a person who steps into a leadership role because they think it will improve their status or social standing or for the perks they think it brings. These individuals will usually be found out and not last long.

Summary: Things to do to make a great first impression in your first 90 days:-

- Show that you believe in your team, push them out of their comfort zones to do challenging tasks but be there to support them so they don't fail, or they can make minor mistakes and learn from them.

- Listen to them when you have your first 1:1 with them.

- Don't micromanage

- Work out your priorities and what you need to start, stop or continue as a team.

CHAPTER 6

CULTURE CLUB

There have been many theories about organisational culture. Here's what I think it shouldn't be about:-

- The way things are done around here and you must fit in to this

- Putting bad buzzwords in posters around the workplace and calling them "values" e.g. "integrity" "Teamwork" "Innovation" Etc. Then using them to point out "red flag" style behaviours to people.

Here's what it should be:-

- The way your organisation makes people feel. Whether that's customers, suppliers or employees.

- How your people feel on a Sunday night about coming into work on Monday morning.

As Brigitte Hyacinth says (www.brigittehyacinth.com)

"Great Leadership isn't about control, it's about empowering people".

I've worked in organisations where the Manager preferred it if everyone with a question formed an orderly queue at their desk and then kept coming back to ask for more help rather than helping them to think things through for themselves. I didn't last too long in that environment...

Case Study 2: Thanks to a member of one of my networking groups for sharing this with me and allowing me to use it in this book.

"At the time I was working in the Insurance industry for a large insurer in town as an Underwriter. Within a few days of starting the role I was given new tasks, including in an area which was not my field of expertise. Therefore it took a while to pick up some of this. My line manager made it clear I was not allowed to make any mistakes. However, I was "drawn over hot coals" early on for not knowing things. My preferred style of learning is on the job. I was micro managed. I wasn't allowed the freedom to learn and do things. It had to be done his way even though was coming in to a specific job. The Management style was very much about looking over my shoulder. My boss was known as "the meerkat". I felt under a lot of pressure. Because I didn't want to say the wrong thing I hated the phone ringing knowing I'd be listened to, so this started to make me anxious. Over the years things got pettier and pettier. I was blamed for other people's mistakes if he hadn't realised others had made them. This was for things like being 1p out on a policy premium.

Other things which I experienced included:-

- Favouritism towards other members of staff

- Being excluded from workplace conversations because it didn't fit my manager's way of doing things.

- Raising it with the Managing Director who refused to listen and wanted to "protect his own"

I ended up raising an unsuccessful grievance and was offered a package to leave. I felt that the HR team didn't have much say or influence and were trying to toe the Company line."

My comments on the above situation is that there are always two sides to every story and in this case I've only heard one side but the situation is one I have come across time and time again during my HR career where companies don't want to acknowledge that there's a problem with an individual manager. If you over micromanage your team they will become paranoid, which means they are more likely to make mistakes, or be disengaged if they don't feel they have ownership over their work. People work better if they have problems to solve and are trusted. All too often good employees leave rather than raise a complaint against a "robust" style of management. The ex employee in question in this case study advised me this happened to them some 10 years ago but it was clear from speaking to them that this was still very fresh in their mind and had a long lasting impact on their self-esteem.

The risk to Companies for allowing this style of management to go on unchallenged is not just a reputational one, but there is also a risk of constructive dismissal claims as well as Personal Injury claims if an individual can prove that their situation got so bad they had no choice but to resign from their role and it's had a lasting impact on their mental health and wellbeing.

So this leads me onto my next tip:-

Tip 3: Don't micromanage. Trust people until they give you a reason not to. Then deal with any situations that need to be dealt with quickly.

Any culture good or bad, starts from the top down so it's important that the Board and the CEO/Managing Director and their Senior Management Team are seen to be behaving in the right way so others follow that lead. Behaviour breeds Behaviour.

A good example of this was the 2022 "partygate" scandal which engulfed the Tory government about parties taking place when social distancing lockdown measures were in place. The Sue Gray report concluded that the culture of an organisation is set from the top down. So it's important that any senior leadership team recognises this and leads by example.

A good culture can be the difference between someone leaving your organisation and going to a competitor for more money/better benefits, or staying put because they feel they're making a difference, their ideas are listened to and they feel a sense of belonging to something. No amount of extra salary or benefits will make up for being in a toxic culture where people don't want to stay.

At the time of writing this book, it's 2023 and we are in a competitive candidate driven market and sometimes a good culture is all a company can offer if it cannot afford to match the salary and benefits of its competitors.

Without the right people who are motivated a business will fail.

So how can you make sure you create a good culture in your team?-

- Lead from the top – lead by example

- Check in regularly with team members on a 1:1 basis and see how they're doing

- Make sure their ideas are listened to. Even if they can't be taken on, explain why

- Give people problems to solve rather than a long task list of things to do

- Give them autonomy over their work – when and how they carry it out. There's often more than one way to get to a solution.

- Say well done when things go right, give constructive feedback in a timely way when they don't.

Culture – Getting it right

- I've read many different definitions around the meaning of organisational culture but one which sums it up well is "culture is about how your employees feel on Sunday night about coming into work on a Monday morning."

- I've touched on this previously in this book (chapter 3) but I wanted to take a moment to define why this is so important to get right no matter how big the business is and whether you're managing staff at Team Leader or C Suite level.

- Many organisations will have a vision/mission statement about why they exist. If you're a CEO of a start up this may just be in your head, but something will drive a business owner or Managing Director to lead an organisation. Do they want to make the world a better place? Are they pushing an amazing product or service they believe will make people's lives better?

- From that mission/vision, particularly in larger organisations will come some "core values". These are defined as principles/beliefs that an organisation sees as being important. The issue that often comes up with values is they become nothing more than pretty looking posters on the wall in a reception area. If people don't know what they are, remember them, believe in them they become meaningless. They can also become very generic. Two thirds of the top FTSE 100 companies to work for had very similar values e.g. integrity, teamwork/collaboration, trust etc. Whilst these are important, values really need to reflect what people are thinking in the organisation at the time and say something that makes that organisation unique and will entice people to want to come and work there, and stay there, at least for a bit. For me, integrity and teamwork should be a given!

• The values an organisation has, lives, and creates should also be easy to remember and reflected in everything that is carried out – whether that's hiring new employees, to how clients/customers/service users are treated, to how the senior leadership team/board conduct themselves.

• Make no mistake, introducing Indian Head Massages or giving people free fruit/pizza/gym membership isn't going to solve a potential toxic culture problem.

Sarah McLellan in her newsletters "Make it Human" talks about ten signs of culture cracks in an organisation. All these are red flags and ones that if you see them happening where you are, call them out. Thankfully, all of them are fixable if you as leaders have the right mindset:-

1. Success is measured through hours worked and long hours are seen as a badge of honour

2. Double Standards where leaders don't follow their own rules, leading to resentment and mistrust

3. Frozen Core – Managers are frozen by process and chains of approval leading to stifling ideas, creativity, development and engagement.

4. Silence – If people can't say what they are thinking it suggests people don't feel psychologically safe and blocks belonging and inclusion

5. Culture Clouds – Accepting toxic behaviours from individuals because they deliver results

6. Parent/Child – Sugar coating messages and making decisions on other's behalf's leads to dependency and resentment

7. Hero Complex – Over reliance on a small group of caped crusaders saving the day can divide rather than strengthen the workforce.

8. Corporate Clones – Bringing in old pals through the back door, building teams who all appear the same narrows influences and innovation

9. History Lessons – Too much focus on the past stops transformation especially when external voices are excluded

10. Profit over purpose – if the main metric for success is financial you risk alienating teams and cutting short your Company's existence.

And the top 5 biggest culture killers are given as:-

1. Leaders playing favourites, overlooking poor behaviour for 'star' performers

2. Being hampered by the past… 'We tried that, it failed'

3. Success = only financial results

4. Managers frozen by bureaucracy

5. Fear of sharing honest feedback and encountering silence in meetings

Culture also goes way beyond just a good "employee experience" – hence my last comment about Indian Head massages. Culture aka "the way you do things" impacts every part of your business including your relationship with the buyers of your products and services. And having "values" won't make employees change their behaviour accordingly overnight, you need to change your culture – and you need to know what you want it to be. This is not something which is "HR's job" alone. A consultant like me can help you do it, by helping you to work out what's really going on in a workplace and how to change it, but ultimately these changes has to be owned by everyone in a Company and you as a manger need to be promoting it and leading it. Don't just have a few "change and culture champions" to do that either – it's complete BS. **You as a people leader need to own this stuff.**

CHAPTER 7

STEPPING UP TO BEING A NEW PEOPLE LEADER

The tips in here apply regardless of whether you are about to be promoted internally or if you're coming into a team as a manager from another organisation.

Before Starting, but after the offer is made

- Meet up with the senior manager you will report into for an informal chat in or outside of your new workplace and find out more about your new team.

- Ask if there's any reading/homework/anything you need to be doing/working on before you start in the role

- If possible, drop into work and meet your new team before you start (or over a Teams/Zoom call depending on how hybrid the new work environment is)

During your first few days/week

- Have 1:1's with all your team members. Find out what their job involves, what they enjoy, what they don't, current challenges they're facing.

- Make your expectations clear but also ask them how they like to be managed – this will really help you adapt your style early on to get the best out of each person.

- Check in with your own manager, give early initial thoughts/observations/questions. Find out if there's anything key that they would like you to focus on in those first few weeks/months.

- Learn any new internal systems/processes you need to

- Identify the culture of the team and the wider company. Note any big "do's" or "don'ts"

- Start to devise a to do list of what needs to be done. Split this up in to short, mid and long term goals otherwise you may become overwhelmed with trying to do everything at once.

- Have intro meetings with any other key contacts in other teams in the organisation who you will be working closely with. Get feedback on your team and how they're perceived in the organisation.

- Have clear, concise meetings with a sense of purpose and clear outcomes that don't waste time.

The managers I feel sorry for are the ones who are promoted internally. I was one of those for my first manager role in my 20's. It's not easy to go from being a colleague to stepping up to be someone's manager. Relationships will change, and should. You can't always be everyone's friend all the time and you may have to have difficult conversations with people who were once at the same level as you. Work out how you will adapt to having these different types of relationships before your promotion takes effect. Also, just because you know the organisation and the people still doesn't mean you'll be a great manager automatically – you still need to implement the above points.

How do you like to be managed?

This is a very personal thing and will vary from individual to individual. For me I like to know a manager is there for advice/support/a second opinion if I need one, and will back me up when I've done the right thing and someone still complains. Otherwise, I'm happy to be given a problem to solve and trusted to get on with it, but know they are there for guidance.

The worst thing a manager could do for me which would make me want to quit would be: Not listen to any of my ideas or claim them as their own, refuse to change, micromanage me, talk to me like I'm a naughty child, or exclude me from key meetings/pieces of information that have been shared with the rest of the team. And if I've done something wrong, not tell me there and then but save it up for the appraisal meeting.

You also need to think carefully about how you mange different types of employee: here's a few tips based on the different types of people you meet in the workplace.

The Apprentice

Typically, these people will be straight out of school or college and won't understand the world of work, your workplace culture, and what they have to do, and what is and isn't acceptable. You need to put extra time aside to support these people, rather than hoping that paying them the minimum wage will save your salary bill and they'll just pick it up. Some will, but many won't. And if they quit, you're back to the drawing board again.

You need to design a good comprehensive training programme for them and not assume a certain level of knowledge that you would get from someone joining you from another Company.

The graduate

Graduate jobs are different now to what they were. There are still a few companies which offer graduates a scheme when they join from university, do a rotation of placements within the Company for a year or so, and then are/aren't guaranteed a job at the end of it. These places are few, and the interest high so typically many graduates will do what I did – start at the bottom of a Company's hierarchy and work their way up, and change between companies depending on where the opportunities are. Even if someone is in a role which they are over qualified for on paper, make sure that they do it well, and when they do, give them other development opportunities to keep them engaged and their brain ticking over. But also be sure to manage their expectations – they won't necessary be promoted to the CEO's position within a year or two as many seem to think!

The plodder

Please don't be too offended by this heading if you recognise yourself in this category. This is for those people who are happy to come into their role on a day-to-day basis, at any level within the organisation – do it well, and then go home again. They have little ambition to want to climb the career ladder. That's ok! You can't have a company with too many ambitious people in, but also you can't have one with too many plodders either – you need a mix of both. The key with these people is that whilst they are likely to be solid and dependable, you need to make sure that firstly they can adapt to change if the organisation evolves, and secondly that they continue to develop their skills and knowledge and not just carry on as they were because that's the way they've been doing their job since they started it in the year dot.

The rival internal candidate who didn't get your job

It can be difficult if you and another internal candidate both went for the same promotion, you got the position but they didn't. You will need to establish a relationship with them still, particularly if you are now managing them! For me, it's important here to not just pretend the interview process never happened, but ask them how they are feeling, and make sure that if they're still keen to develop and have the potential to do so that you give them the right development opportunities so they don't feel they are stagnating in their role. If they act in a more disruptive way towards you as they are upset they didn't get the job, then you will need to have that difficult conversation with them about manner and attitude.

The go getter who will stand on your head to get above you/others

A bit like the rival candidate above, there are people in an organisation who want to get ahead and develop (which is great) but at the same time you need to make sure that they are not doing it at the detriment or expense of others. If you notice any political behaviour it's important that you call this out, find out from the individual exactly what they're looking for and help them find a more appropriate way of getting this, assuming what they want is acceptable.

And a quick word here about Employment Status

I could write a whole book on this topic so I'll keep this simple but the point I want to make is that in the UK there are three types of employment status, and it's important that you know which is which if you have a team consisting of more than one type. If you're ever unsure about what someone's employment status might be, please don't guess or leave it to chance – ask an HR professional.

- Type 1 – Employee. Paid via payroll with various rights depending on length of service.

- Type 2 – Worker. Also typically paid via payroll, has less rights than an employee. These individuals often work on a casual/nil hours type of contract where there's no obligation to be offered/accept work.

- Type 3 – Self employed. Either as a sole trader or through their own limited Company. No employment rights, although your Health and Safety at work legislation and Data Protection Legislation will apply to them as it will to your Workers and Employees too. Typically taken on for a project or a retained basis as a subject expert.

It's always important to avoid unlimited fines and prison sentences to make sure that you check that someone is legally entitled to work in the UK and that you evidence these checks have taken place. For those who are self employed you also need to get proof of their self employed status and see a copy of their liability insurance.

Finally, you need to treat these groups of people differently. Self employed should not be treated the same way as employees. The reason for this is if there is ever a dispute, a judge at a tribunal will ignore the paperwork, look at what happens in reality and could therefore decide one of your "contractors" is actually an employee based on how you've been treating them.

PART TWO:

HOW TO MANAGE YOUR TEAM THROUGH THE EMPLOYEE LIFECYCLE

The employee lifecycle = everything that an individual can encounter during their time with you. From applying for a position as an external candidate, through to being offered a role, being employed and eventually leaving an organisation.

CHAPTER 8

GROWING YOUR TEAM

One thing many managers will have to do is recruit their own team members, either because the team is expanding or to replace someone who's left. It's much more than just looking through some CV's and picking the one you like the best.

I've recruited consistently throughout my HR career. Sometimes as the independent HR panel members, sometimes as the line manager or senior manager of the team. The first person I ever recruited went onto win several internal awards for excellence. I thought to myself then, "if everyone is as good as that, I've got this in the bag". However, not everyone I've recruited has worked out as well. We all get it wrong sometimes. Sometimes the personality on display at interview is very different to the person who actually turns up to work on the first day. That's ok, provided you act on your mistakes quickly and learn from them.

Here are some key tips so you as the employer/potential future manager don't end up looking like a dick to the candidates. Some of these you may not be able to control directly, but you could speak to your MD/Marketing Person to start to put these measures in place.

Get the hiring pages on your Company's website right

Many Company websites are the first places a potential candidate comes to when deciding whether or not they want to work for your Company. So first impressions are important! Make it easy for them to apply by having a welcoming, easy to navigate careers section. I strongly recommend working with a Marketing Manager to help get the brand and the copy right. So many companies focus on their website just being about attracting customers to buy their product or service but I think it's equally important to market yourselves to the pool(s) of candidates that you are trying to attract for your roles. Think about where they hang out, what they're into, what social media they use, what they care about, what motivates them, and - what would make them want to actually come and work for you? You can do this by coming up with a fictional named individual, or individuals and doing this exercise for them. It's an exercise often used by marketers for helping them pitch to their ideal customers, so I suggest using it to think about who your ideal candidate is, and write the website copy, the adverts, and the description in a language that they're going to relate to.

Get the job description right

So many people I've worked with in the past have seen the job description / job profile / role profile, or whatever your Company is calling it as another HR tick box exercise. But for me, this is an important document because without it, how will you know what you're looking for and what you want your role to be doing?

I always advise hiring managers to be realistic, not to try and spend years trying to recruit the "golden unicorn" e.g. an endless search for the perfect candidate that doesn't exist because the skills set being asked for doesn't exist, or at least not in the way that you think you want it to.

Traditional job descriptions tend to be a list of duties followed by a "person specification" e.g. list of previous experience and qualifications required for the role and whether they are "essential" or "desirable".

I'd suggest writing them differently. Try focussing instead on outputs than endless tasks and be realistic about the qualifications and experience. I also suggest moving away from saying "5 years experience in XYZ disciplines" as you can have 20 years experience and be rubbish, versus having 2 years experience and being amazing! You don't want to put good quality candidates off applying, but also you don't want to encourage people to apply who don't have the right experience, particularly if you've got a niche role.

You can then use this document not only to benchmark your pool of candidates against, but also to measure performance once your successful candidate is in the role.

Nothing frustrates a candidate more when you don't actually know what you're looking for and you delay things or are constantly changing your mind. Would someone want to come and work for you if you are that indecisive?

Get the job advert right

This is your opportunity to sell the role, the organisation you work for, and to be clear and concise about what you want. A traditional, advert may look like this:-

Salary: Competitive

Applications are invited from suitably qualified individuals to work in our Customer Service Centre. Reporting directly into the Customer Services Manager you will be responsible for ensuring our customers receive good service, and the Manager is kept updated at all times around the team's SLA's.

To succeed in this role you will have:-

At least 5 years experience in a similar role

Experience of supervising a small team of customer service advisors

Ability to present reports/statistics using a variety of methods

Proven Microsoft Office experience

To apply, please go to www.anycompany.com/careers and download our application pack.

For an informal discussion only please telephone Mr Jones, Customer Services Manager on 01234 654321.

Whilst there's nothing illegal about this advert that's likely to get you into trouble, how much better and more appealing/personal does it sound if you write it like this instead?

Of course, a lot depends on your culture as to how you want to write your adverts too. If you're more of a traditional organisation you don't want your marketing to make you out to be something you're not as the candidates will not get the employee experience they were expecting when they signed up. However, as you can see from the adverts there are some key differences between the two styles.

Customer Services Supervisor

£25,000 per annum, for 37.5 hours per week on a rota basis from 8am – 9pm Monday-Friday working one Saturday in four.

Are you passionate about giving good customer service? Can you motivate a small team and report on statistics? If so we'd like to hear from you.

Due to an internal promotion, we are looking for a Customer Services Supervisor to join our team. Your role will be to act as a role model, to train and develop the Customer Service Advisors and to make sure that the team meet their service level agreements.

If you have proven experience in a call centre or dealing with customers over the telephone, and can show you have what it takes to manage a team and present KPI's then you will enjoy this role.

In addition to the salary offered, we also offer hybrid working and a bonus scheme linked to the team meeting their service agreements.

To apply, please go to www.anycompany.com/careers and download our application pack.

For an informal discussion only please telephone Steve Jones, Customer Services Manager on 01234 654321.

No Agencies please

- I've mentioned some of the key company benefits

- I've mentioned the hours to save candidates asking, so they don't apply if they can't work a rota or weekends.

- I've mentioned the salary! Please never write "competitive" in your salary adverts. After all, no one buys a car if the banner on the dashboard reads "competitive". A new job is potentially life changing, and people need to know that if they take up your offer they can afford to live/commute on the salary you're offering, as well as work the job around any other commitments.

- I've written the second advert in a more friendly, welcoming tone and hinted that the company offers career progression.

- I've kept it brief- if people are scrolling through ads on job boards, they will have a short attention span so what you're saying needs to stand out.

- I've removed the number of years experience and replaced it with "proven experience"

Don't discriminate

Sounds straight forward enough, but many hiring managers will have what's called "unconscious bias." This is defined as **"social stereotypes about certain groups of people that individuals form outside their own conscious awareness**. Everyone holds unconscious beliefs about various social and identity groups, and these biases stem from one's tendency to organize social worlds by categorizing." (Source: https://diversity.ucsf.edu/) Therefore it's important to make sure that when hiring you look to get the best person for the job and don't chose them for the wrong reasons.

It's so important to write a job description in a way that doesn't inadvertently discriminate against people due to protected characteristics such as age ("graduate that must have 10 years experience"), gender ("workmanship" "Chairman"), disability ("must have a driving licence") LGBTQ+ (e.g. using "she/he" rather than "them/their"). Again, if you're unsure ask an HR professional for help. There are also some great online tools that help you make sure your advert isn't accidentally gender biased, such as https://gender-decoder. katmatfield.com/

Mrs Smith or Mrs Singh?

There's a well known tribunal case where the same individual applied for the same job twice using identical application forms and processes. The only difference was they used an English sounding name on one application and a non English name on the other. "Mrs Smith" got shortlisted for an interview "Mrs Singh" did not. The applicant who was from a non UK background took the company advertising the role to an employment tribunal and won their case, even though they were not an employee. This proves just how important it is to not discriminate consciously or otherwise during a recruitment process.

Don't sit around – move fast or lose great candidates!

So many hiring managers wonder why candidates drop out of the process quickly or have other offers, and they have to spend time going back to the drawing board when working on a recruitment campaign. Here's the blunt truth of it for you – candidates are not obligated to wait for you to try and shortlist your job around your other commitments. Chances are, they will be applying for other roles too and at the time of writing, it's a fast moving candidate market.

So don't wait! Move quickly! I can't make this point enough. Most campaigns I know of in recent years fail because the hiring manager doesn't look through the CV's fast enough and are indecisive. Many like to sit on a few CV's they think look ok in the hope "a comparator" or "to see what else is out there". Trust me, it gets very messy if you have candidates all at different stages of the process e.g. you've interviewed someone at stage 1 but still have an ad running in case there's someone else and someone else has had a stage 2 interview.

Just work through defined key timescales and plan your campaign ahead. Don't go on holiday if you've got a campaign running, don't interview if you have other key work meetings going on at the same time. I'd suggest something like this

- Before Go Live: Get job description and advert written/updated, seek internal authorisation if needed, plan the budget needed and agree timescales and which job board(s)/social media you want your advert to go on

- Put the role live – close applications 10-14 days later or once you reach 20-30 applications, you decide.

- Don't look to hire if you're on holiday or have lots of key meetings going on.

- Shortlist straight away – as you receive applications

- Send out not shortlisted e mails (or using your applicant tracking system to do this) straight away for those not selected for interview so they know. It's better than being left wondering.

- Invite successful candidates to interview. Agree in advance if you are having a 1 or a 2 stage process and if you want to include any other selection methods. Make a phone call and follow up on e mail.

- Hold your interviews. Be realistic with candidates when you will make a decision by.

- Phone the successful candidate to make the offer, send unsuccessful e mails to the remaining candidates.

- Offer constructive feedback if requested.

- Close the process off. If you're doing it right it should be done within around 8 weeks from an advert going live to you making the offer and issuing the new starter paperwork.

IN a 2022 BCG Survey, 90,547 respondents answered a survey which gives some great insights into what's motivating talent depending on age. Something to consider depending on the demographic of your workforce. From this you can see flexible work location/schedule and work life balance are really important so as a People Leader you need to get these things right.

WHAT IS MOTIVATING TALENT

<21	21 - 30	31 - 40	41 - 50	51 - 60	>60
Work-life Balance	Financial Compensation	Financial Compensation	Financial Compensation	Work-life Balance	Impactful or Meaningful Work
Financial Compensation	Work-life Balance	Work-life Balance	Work-life Balance	Financial Compensation	Appreciation of Ones Work
Career Learning Opportunities	Amount of Annual & Paid Leave	Job Security	Job Security	Relationship With Manager	Financial Compensation
Appreciation of Ones Work	Job Security	Flexible Work Location & Schedule	Flexible Work Location & Schedule	Appreciation of Ones Work	Relationship With Manager
Flexible Work Location & Schedule	Flexible Work Location & Schedule	Amount of Annual & Paid Leave	Relationship With Manager	Alignment of Company & Personal Values	Alignment of Company & Personal Values

Ask the right questions/Have a human conversation

I hope you would know already that it's illegal to ask someone if they're planning to start a family any time soon as part of a hiring process, or after! The interview should be more of a relaxing conversation these days than an interrogation. As the interviewer you should only do about 20% of the talking. Talk about the role, the Company, sell the position to them but ask sensible questions based around the tasks and experience you've asked for in the job description that will tell you whether

- The candidate can do the job and

- That you can work with them

So many candidates are very experienced at answering competency-based interview questions (questions based on the job description) which is why I suggest having some behavioural questions in there as well as these are harder to second guess.

If you relax and make it sound like a human conversation rather than you behaving like a robot and asking a series of structured questions "because HR told you to" the candidate is more likely to relax and tell you things than they would do otherwise, and you're more likely to get a real flavour of what they're really like. Meaning you're less likely to hire the wrong person!

Make the right offer

You've hopefully been transparent about all your company benefits and salary on the job advert/company website, so when you phone the candidate to offer don't penny pinch by offering them something less than advertised as it will instantly make them feel devalued. Also know if you offer something verbally it is legally binding so be careful to also not offer something that you can't deliver on (like a payrise guarantee in 6 months' time). If a candidate rejects you because they've had a better offer (sadly this happens now) see if you have a good second choice you can offer to. It makes commercial sense to hold back on giving the outcome to a second strong candidate if they are capable of doing the job too until you know for sure if the first choice has accepted or rejected your offer. But also don't act out of desperation and live to regret it. If you don't have a strong second choice go back to the drawing board, and use the opportunity to consider why the first campaign didn't work.

Make sure they're legal

You can end up in prison and with an unlimited fine if you employ someone illegally in the UK. Therefore make sure you carry out the correct proof of right to work in the UK checks before employment begins. Don't just assume because someone has a British sounding name that they have an automatic right to work in the UK either. For advice on the current rules around checks look at https://www.gov.uk/view-right-to-work

Probation

In the employment contract, Probation is often written as a two way trial period – in other words, "are we right for each other".

The concept is a useful one when used correctly e.g. if either party, the employee or employer feels that it's not working out, either side can usually give a shorter notice period than after probation has been passed. I would encourage companies who want to continue to have such a period to see if they can find a more welcoming sounding name! Secondly, the period should be used for regular informal check ins and making expectations known, not just seen as a paperwork exercise that will keep HR happy. If it is, you need to have a serious rethink! Some companies have abolished the probationary period altogether – although for this to work it doesn't mean a manager should just show the employee to their desk/workstation/company van etc and leave them to get on with it- they still need to have a solid onboarding programme.

Ultimately, in the UK you can exit an employee with under two years' service without the risk of an unfair dismissal claim provided you are not discriminating against them, follow the correct dismissal process and have evidence to prove where things have gone wrong and where you've tried to support. I will often help Companies write this into their contracts and handbooks so that there is a longer period to monitor performance that avoids going through a lengthy formal process if there are performance or behavioural issues that occur.

If you really insist on having one then use it well, and make sure you check in regularly with the new hire to make sure they

- Understand what's expected of them

- Feel they can raise queries/concerns/issues quickly, (as can you)

- Feel they are part of the team, department and Company

However if there are issues which arise after the probationary period has been passed, don't wait until the eleventh hour before dealing with them – best to start before 18 months service is reached.

Onboarding

Again, this should not be just a checklist that's returned to HR and sits on someone's file to prove that they've undertaken XY&Z training sessions and claimed to have read, learned and inwardly digested the company handbook! I've yet to see one of these pieces of paper be submitted successfully as tribunal evidence that someone has been trained to the right standard. A good onboarding process should make the new employee feel that they belong to the team from day 1, their contribution is appreciated and they have a voice. This can include some formal and informal training around systems, covering off tours of the site so they know where to eat lunch, where to park their car etc. It's also important that they feel at home before they even join, so it's good to build some things in whilst they are working out a notice period before they join you.

Case Study: don't be like one manager who didn't show a new inexperienced employee around the site on their first day. They didn't know there was a fridge in which to put their lunch, meaning they ate a warm lunch with meat in and gave themselves food poisoning. The manager then complained that they had been off sick with said food poisoning. The manager believed that was HR's role rather than theirs to do that.

Also, don't deliver a dry, lengthy corporate induction where everyone is bored by a succession of PowerPoint presentations. It's good to know a bit about the Company history and meet key people but better to do this in a more interactive, fun way than how many organisations have historically done this.

How good an onboarding programme is, relates to how the employee feels at the end of it in terms of how they belong to the Company and feel part of it. Not how many boxes get ticked.

Get all of the above right and hopefully you're far less likely to have issues with your employees and you are more likely to have the right people working for you, and to the right standard. Ask your HR department if you have one, as they may have already created onboarding and induction processes so you don't have to reinvent the wheel, but you may also need to add any department/team specific training into that.

Case Study 2: This one actually happened to me. My new manager forgot I was starting and wasn't present on my first day at all as they thought I was starting a week later even though I definitely turned up in the right place/time as stated in my offer letter. Didn't make me feel great and I spent a few weeks browsing the intranet and reading policies before I was then just thrown in at the deep end and left to get on with the job.

CHAPTER 9

HANDLING DIFFICULT SITUATIONS

OK, so no matter how much you may have tried to apply some of these ideas there may just be one or two people in your team who you may have to have a difficult conversation with.

In the words of Perry Belcher, the Co-Founder of Digital-Marketer.com,

"Nothing will kill a great employee faster than watching you tolerate a bad one".

Sometimes there will be that one employee who just doesn't want to come with you on the journey that you want to which improves things. Reasons for this could include

- They've been allowed to coast under a previous manager so feel threatened if someone competent is starting to look closely at what they do and can see through them.

- They are mistaking being correctly managed for "bullying". But make sure that you're not actually bullying them!

- They want an easy life and are scared about having to think or do things differently to the "way that they've always been done"

- They feel threatened by you

The key here is to act quickly, and professionally and not be afraid to have that tricky conversation. Other topics which you may have to cover include but are not limited to: High levels of sickness absence, persistent lateness, under performance, poor appearance/body odour, acting unprofessionally. It's also important to remember as the people leader you are not their parent and they are still an adult. If you know the individual and know what is likely to make them respond in the right way you can prepare what you want to say in advance. As this is not an exam you are allowed to make notes and have examples to hand of what you want to say – but do it quickly as the longer you leave it, the less relevant it will appear.

Underperforming – Don't move around the issue – sort it out!

Over the years, I've seen some managers promote poorly performing people into other roles in the hope that they will "step up" and take the responsibility. In every case I've seen this has failed as these things rarely motivate an individual to change their behaviour. It's also sending the wrong message to others e.g. poor performance and behaviour will get you promoted. Almost every time I've been called into try and help either performance manage or exit those individuals. Moving a "problem" employee from post A to post B never solves the issues.

So what do you do with a poorly performing individual? (Whether that's performance or behaviour)

- Look for signs and patterns – is the performance suddenly taking a dip? Could there be reasons for this inside or outside of the workplace? Is there any change in behaviour? Make sure you pick up on non verbal signs too.

- Have examples to hand, this could be in e mail evidence or just observations you've made

- Act quickly – don't bring up incidents for the first-time weeks or months after they've happened.

- Be empathetic, particularly if the person has not been like this in the past.

- Prepare what you're going to say in advance and bring notes into the meeting with you if you need to – it's not an exam!

You then need to get them into a meeting, usually this would be an informal meeting in the first instance unless it's serious misconduct or performance.

Here's how to do it:-

- Find a convenient location where neither of you will be overheard or seen.

- Explain that you would like to have a talk to them about a recent incident/issue and give details.

- Ask them what their recollection is of the situation and if their perception is different to yours. Take their response into account and see if it changes anything you want to say.

- Make it clear what your expectations are about what is expected in the future

- Make sure your tone and language remains calm and non-accusatory throughout.

- Ask if they need any support to make the changes which are needed

- Make it clear what could happen if they fail to improve

- Document the conversation and follow it up as a summary e mail (That way if you need to take a more formal approach in the future you have an audit trail)

Usually, saying the right thing in the right way at the right time is enough to stop difficult situations escalating further. But do nothing, or hope it will go away by itself could leave you exposed and open to criticism from the rest of your team.

Using one of my all time favourite quotes from the BBC Sitcom "My Family"

"If you bury your head in the sand, all people see is an arsehole".

Having these types of conversations is an art, and hopefully something you won't have to do very often but the more you do them, the more confident you become.

Tip 4: You always have a right to manage your staff, but do it in the right way to avoid successful grievances (or union intervention)

Do's	Don'ts
Keep yourself up to date with what's happening in your team Recognise issues and tackle them early on before they escalate. Be a human being and make sure you present as one to your team! Know they can approach you and you'll take a non judgemental approach to what they talk to you about. Gather evidence to support what you're saying before you tackle an issue. Document everything so you have a written record to use Listen to your team and adapt your style to get the best out of each of your team members. Be prepared to adapt to change and alter your perspective on the world as things do.	Appear to act like you know it all and your team know nothing e.g. "my way or the highway". It's ok to not know, find out the answer and revert! Think issues will magically resolve themselves. Give your team members a dressing down in a public place causing embarrassment. Not listen to the feedback your team are giving you. Act in an authoritarian style.

Dress Code

I wanted to put something about a workplace's dress code in this book as many of my clients often ask me for advice around this. This could have equally sat under "Culture" but I've put it here as a "difficult situation" because it is a delicate matter, and it's one where I think Managers need to be aware of how to handle.

Most companies will have an official or unofficial dress code – that is, their expectations about what you will wear to work. Some Companies will have their own uniform or logo branded clothing that they expect people to wear. It should be obvious from the culture about what is acceptable and what isn't. Some workplaces still remain quite traditional and formal whilst others are more casual unless the roles are client facing.

Dress is also a sensitive matter with cultural/religious variances as well. Also employees will have their own views on what they feel comfortable wearing.

What I don't recommend doing is having a lengthy, specific policy on dress code which no one will read anyway and gets added to in a passive aggressive manner every time someone wears something which someone else takes to be unacceptable. Or an extra line is added to it after one unique case of someone wearing something inappropriate.

It is also not the job of your HR department to be the fashion police and send out passive aggressive e mails reminding people of the correct attire to be worn if one person is seen to be wearing something that's "unusual".

I've upset various managers in my career (sorry, not sorry!) by telling them that if someone is wearing something that's not appropriate it's **their** job to take their direct report to one side, and have a quiet/difficult conversation with them, not that of the HR person.

The best dress code policies I've seen are very simple and say things like "dress for your day" and also "If you look in the mirror and ask yourself "can I get away with wearing this" and the answer is no, then you should probably change. (Source:- "Disruptive HR")

CHAPTER 10

MANAGING ABSENCES... AND PRESENTEEISM

One of the most common issues a manager may come across is absenteeism from the team. This could be due to a number of reasons including Holiday, Sickness (long and short term), Bereavement, Doctors/Dentists/Opticians Appointments, Emergency childcare/sickness issues and poor weather. Typically, your organisation should have specific policies in place for these situations. If not, then I would suggest these are created so that everyone is treated consistently, fairly, and everyone knows what's expected and also how much time off is appropriate, and how much of it, if any should be paid or unpaid.

Therefore what follows is an overview of these types of absence and advice for best practice.

Holiday

Every UK employee is entitled to a statutory minimum of 28 days holiday (5.6 weeks) per year including bank holidays. Many companies may choose to give more, or increase entitlement with length of service. Whilst some companies will allow untaken holiday to be carried forward from one leave year to the next, it is not legally possible to allow people to do this when their entitlement is at the statutory minimum. (e.g. 20 days + 8 bank holidays if full time and in England/Wales)

For part time employees, their holiday entitlement should be "pro rata'd" down accordingly. Here's where it's important to know how many hours make up a full time week. For example:-

If a full time week is 37.5 hours and John is contracted to work 22.5 hours (regardless of the actual pattern of when these are worked) his holiday entitlement would be 60% of what a full timer's would be e.g. 28 days x 0.6 = 16.8 days. If an employer wishes, for ease, entitlement may be rounded up to the nearest half day or day, so in this case 17 days. It's not legal to round it down.

I would suggest that part timers always have their holiday in hours rather than days so if their working pattern is variable or they work fewer hours per day, it's easier to deduct the right amount.

Using John as an example. His 22.5 hours are worked

- Monday 7.5 hours

- Tuesday 8 hours

- Wednesday 7 hours

- Thursday – Non working day

- Friday – Non working day

Therefore a "day" for him is of unequal value. Meaning if his holiday is in hours if he wants a Monday off 7.5 hours are deducted from his entitlement, if a Tuesday 8 hours etc.

Whilst many HR systems will calculate this for you, it's important that you understand the logic around how these are calculated as you may get asked by your employee!

Bank Holidays

A contract of employment should state whether Bank Holidays are considered to be normal working days or not. I'm often asked by clients what the entitlement should be for a part timer whose working days don't fall on bank holidays.

The answer = exactly the same as someone who is part time and working days **do** fall on bank holidays.

Final point here, legally in the UK employees must take a minimum of 28 days holiday each year including the 8 bank holidays although some Companies will offer more. This was temporarily changed during the pandemic but has now reverted back to the original position. If you only give people the statutory minimum, then no carry forward should be allowed. As the manager, it's your job to make sure that your team take all the leave that's owing to them. After all, they're being paid to not come into work – so make sure they take the time off to relax as they will come back more refreshed and hopefully more motivated.

Case Study: Jack and Jill

Jack and Jill both work part time at AnyCompany Ltd. Their full time week is 40 hours, and both are contracted to work 20 hours a week each.

Jack works all day Mondays and Tuesdays and Wednesday morning, Jill works Wednesday afternoon and all day Thursdays and Fridays.

Both of them are entitled to 224 hours of leave per year pro rata'd down. (e.g. 40 hours per week x 5.6 weeks per year =

224 hours). Actual entitlement is 112 hours each as they both are contracted to work for 50% of a full time week.

Because the majority of UK bank holidays typically fall on a Monday Jack will be required to book all the bank holidays out of his leave entitlement. Alternatively, if you allow it, he could change his working hours for the weeks of the bank holidays and work the hours at another time. However because Jill works the end of the week where typically only 1-2 bank holidays a year may fall those need to be booked as well, but any excess bank holiday entitlement can be taken off at any other time.

Depending on the size of your organisation I highly recommend a good HR Database which will calculate these types of entitlements for you and will allow them to be requested and authorised electronically so you can keep on top of it. If you only have a few employees then a good spreadsheet should suffice.

Sickness – Short Term

Your Organisation should define what is meant by short and long term sickness. Many of my clients have been surprised when I've told them that they can tackle their employees about frequent, short term absence but are unsure on what they can and cannot say. Whilst each case is different my advice would be to carry out a short return to work interview after every period of absence, document this on their file, and point out patterns of absence e.g. every Friday/Monday, same illness reoccurring.

Employees can self certify their sickness absence for up to 7 calendar days, after that they will need a Statement of Fitness for Work.

Initially any concerns about short term absence should be looked at supportively, e.g. is there anything I as a manager can do to help you improve your absence, and are you as the employee doing all you can to improve your absence? However if the patterns persist it is possible to undertake disciplinary action for this, provided the illness is not directly related to pregnancy or a disability.

Always get advice from your HR department or consultant on these types of issues before proceeding if you're unsure.

Sickness – Long Term

This is usually anything over 3-4 weeks in duration, although there are specific conditions which should be treated as long term after 2 weeks. One of which is Stress.

In all cases of long term absence you should keep in touch with the employee, agree the frequency of welfare meetings and document these carefully, but also don't continually harass them either. Usually I would advocate for an early occupational health assessment and doing what you can to support a return to work.

In some cases, if someone is deemed medically unfit to return to their role and all other options have been exhausted such as redeployment, reasonable adjustments etc then it is possible to dismiss someone on the grounds of medical capability.

If you have an employee who has declared a disability (Remember they are not obliged to tell you) then the best thing you can do is have an open and honest conversation with them about it, if they're willing to talk to you and ask them if they need any reasonable adjustments made to the job description to help them carry out their role. The legal definition of a disability under the Equality Act 2010 is if you have **a physical or mental impairment that has a 'substantial' and 'long-term' negative effect on your ability to do normal daily activities**. You are not expected, as a manager to be a medical expert either so you can write to the individual's GP or use an Occupational Health provider if you need further advice. The same would apply if one of your team develops a disability whilst they are employed with you.

Again, always get advice from your HR department or HR Consultant on these types of issues before proceeding if you're unsure.

Interlude: An Interview with a disabled employee

D*oug:* *Thanks for agreeing to talk to me today. Can you start by telling me what types of roles you have undertaken, now and in the past?*

Response: I have worked for two further education colleges, I also run my own business as a Counsellor.

Doug: Can you tell me what your disability is and what impact it has on your life on a daily basis?

Response: I have got fibromyalgia and osteo arthritis and a characteristic of the fibromyalgia is chronic fatigue syndrome. The impact on me is that I'm constantly in pain in different parts of my body which is both draining and exhausting.

The pain aspects I can manage, however the chronic fatigue side is more difficult. For example, I was running a workshop in the morning and by the afternoon I was wiped out, I just wanted to go to sleep. It's important for me that I pace myself – by taking regular rest breaks.

Doug: I can imagine that is very difficult. What reasonable adjustments would you need to have made to a job description so you would be able to successfully carry out your role?

Response: Flexible working hours so I can manage the condition and still work. I currently work for half a week as an employee but what works well for me is that I am able to do my hours anytime. Some weeks I do a bit more but other weeks I will do a bit less. It's good that my Manager trusts me to be honest and manage my own time.

Doug: Absolutely! I have been talking for a while now about how the pandemic made a lot of people realise, myself included, it was a strange concept to work constantly between 9 and 5 every day and that every day would have the same amount of work with it. The reality has always been some days are busier than others, and some people do their best work first thing, others later on.

Response: The pandemic definitely was an agent for change. Whilst there were obviously a lot of downsides, there were some definite positives too. In my role it changed how we worked as our students wanted to engage more in the evenings so we ran workshops later in the day when in the past they would have been in the daytime.

Doug: I'm guessing that also being able to work your hours flexibly has meant that you would take less sickness?

Response: Definitely, I've only had one period of time off sick since I started this role and that was 6 years ago. If I hadn't been able to work flexibly, I have no doubt that my sickness record would have been higher as I would have been fatigued and unable to work.

Doug: Can you give me some examples of organisations you've worked for when you've had a positive employee experience– what made it positive?

On the whole my current employer is really good. Although a lot depends on your actual line manager. I've had line managers here who have been brilliant. They've not questioned anything about my condition, they trust me and know I'm good at my job. They will accept if I can't attend a meeting if my condition flares up someone else will cover it. My Manager cares enough to ask me if I'm pacing myself properly and not over doing it. They understood me as a person, and I appreciate these informal welfare check ins that have taken place.

In the past I have found Occupational Health to be invaluable too as they are able to verify what I've been saying and giving a medical opinion with practical advice to managers.

Doug: How about the other extreme – can you give me some examples of organisations you've worked for where you haven't had such a great employee experience.

I struggled when I was told I had to drive to a work event using a pool car because I found it uncomfortable, and would prefer to use my own car as I buy makes/models that are automatic and are comfortable for me to drive. The reason that was given was that the pool car would be cheaper. The drive was also difficult as I was told I couldn't stay overnight and had to drive a considerable distance in a day. The impact this had on me was that it took me several weeks to recover from the pain this put me in.

I also worked for a department where someone was spreading rumours behind my back that I wasn't ill and I was putting it on. The Managers did track the individuals concerned down and made them apologise but they didn't have the difficult conversation with them that they should have done. For me listening to a forced apology was cringeworthy, I would prefer the individual to understand what they had done wrong, why it was wrong and to mean what they said. At the time it happened I had just returned to work following a period of minor surgery which made it harder. This employer also didn't check in on me and ask if I was OK, but were happy for me to be covering multiple classes at the same time which had an impact on my health.

Also, I had a chair delivered through Access to Work which was set up specifically for me. It didn't help when other peo-

ple sat on it, played with the levers and had to be constantly readjusted back for me.

Doug: Finally, what top tips would you give to a people leader who is employing a person with a disability?

Response:

1. *Managers need to have an open, adult conversation with the person to find out what their condition is, and how it affects them. They should be aware that the same condition can also affect different people in different ways. In other words, don't assume you know everything about their condition because someone else you know has it. They may manage it differently.*

2. *Respect the confidentiality of the individual. They may be happy for you to share information with colleagues to increase understanding but equally they may prefer to keep it quiet. Please ask.*

3. *If someone asks to speak to you, know that they want this to be immediate as they will have probably spent a while building up to feeling they can trust you as the manager enough to speak to them. Disabled employees often put a brave face on things.*

4. *Try hard to use the right terminologies for things. Just ask. We'd rather you did. Don't be afraid to ask. Don't assume*

5. *Remember that not all disabilities are visible – check what people actually need before assuming lots of adjustments which could be more expensive than a simple fix. People are often quite ingenious when it comes to solutions to manage their condition.*

6. *Finally, think about how their actions might make the person feel. If someone is asked rather than told/as-*

sumed it makes them feel more valued. Having a simple, adult conversation is an easy fix.

Doug: Thankyou.

A note about Sick Pay Entitlement

When an employee is off sick, they qualify for statutory sick pay. The current rates and information about how to calculate this are here: https://www.gov.uk/statutory-sick-pay Many companies choose to be more generous and offer company sick pay which is usually so many days or weeks at full pay and/or half pay, before reducing to statutory sick pay only. I would usually advocate having clear wording in the contract about the right to these types of leave and applying the rules consistently rather than just giving it on a discretionary basis to the employees you "like" better than others. That said, I know some employees may take the proverbial but here's where having clear absence management procedures and good return to work interviews can really pay off.

Bereavement

Typically many companies will allow some time off with or without pay to deal with the death of a dependent and time off to attend the funeral. Here's where as a manager you need to be empathetic towards someone's needs but also not just allow them unlimited paid time off. What I would say is not to limit this to just close relatives but base it on the person's relationship with the deceased. For example, some may not be close to their family but have friends who are like family to them and would need more time off.

Doctor/Dentist/Optician

Would usually suggest a short paragraph outlining what a Company's stance is on allowing time off for these and if they are paid or unpaid. As a practical measure, would normally recommend that these are booked in wherever possible at the start/end of the working day or at lunchtime. However if the age of hybrid working it should be OK to book these in at any time so long as you as the manager are aware.

Emergency Childcare/Sickness Issues

As a caring employer you should realise that people will from time to time, have issues beyond their control which involve child/elder care, or other caring responsibilities. This means that it is reasonable to allow a short period of emergency leave for dealing with a sick child/parent or similar. The key thing here is that there is no right to paid time off to do this, so typically these events are unpaid, the time is made up, or the individual takes the time from their holiday entitlement. **These should not be classed as sick leave as that is only applicable for when your employee is sick!**

Poor Weather

Again for people who can undertake hybrid working from home/anywhere this is now less of an issue than it once was. But for those who are unable to get to work due to severe snow or similar I'd recommend that if your place of work remains open then they take unpaid leave, paid holiday or make the time up.

You just need to be aware that legally if you decide to close your premises and you are effectively stopping employees coming to work then they are entitled to the time off paid without having to take holiday or make the time up.

Managing Presenteeism

This part of the book could just have easily been in the "Culture" section, as it's relevant there too. There are many definitions of the term "presenteeism" but for me it refers to when people work excessive hours despite being sick, or similar.

In my first HR job, despite having flexitime I remember being told that it was important I was seen to be at my desk for so many hours per day (even though I didn't actually have enough work to do to fill that time up as I got my head down and got on with the job and I'd worked long into the evening on a project that needed to be done out of hours...) In the same organisation, I remember senior leaders looking out of the window and not leaving until they'd seen that the CEO had left for the day. Not the kind of culture I would want to encourage where people aren't treated like adults and trusted.

It's best thought of like this:-

Sue is a long serving employee with 10 years service who works in the Finance Team and is at her desk by 8.00 a.m. each morning, which is noticed by the Manager as they walk to their desk. She leaves the office after many of her colleagues and is not averse to sending work e mails from home late into the evening.

The Manager thinks that's amazing and admires Sue's commitment. The Manager wishes that more staff showed that amount of dedication rather than just appearing to rush out of the door/turn the laptop off as soon as it gets to 5pm.

The HR person is worried about Sue's mental health and wellbeing as they want to encourage people to "Switch" off outside of work hours and worry that they may be overloaded in their job. When they talk to Sue and ask why they're e mailing late and working long days most days, Sue responds by saying that she's really busy doing ABC then XYZ.

When the HR person observes her more closely they notice that she spends a lot of her day between 9 and 5 going round chatting to other people, telling them how busy she is, and also takes a lot of personal phone calls on her mobile and then browsing the internet.

So it becomes clear to the HR Person that Sue is too busy to actually get work done within the normal business hours.

As an aside, in this type of role that Sue carries out where there are no strict shift patterns attached to it if Sue was neurodiverse and worked better in the evenings than the mornings then it would be a good thing for their Manager + HR to agree a different working pattern to help her. Similarly, a time and motion study would help to establish if the individual is genuinely overwhelmed and if they have taken on too much. Experience teaches me it's difficult for some people to let go of parts of "their" role in a business, so this must be handled sensitively.

However, in this story there is no neurodiversity and the workload is reasonable and the problem we have which I've seen in so many workplaces is that Sue won't be likely to change her working habits because she's getting praise from her manager and perceived to be very committed to the business.

What needs to happen is for the culture to change and for HR to facilitate this by making not just the manager but all senior leaders realise that a good work life balance is a good thing, which increases positive mental health, productivity, and reduces the risk of poor quality work, turnover, negative reviews on Glassdoor/Indeed etc.

So if you notice any Sue's in your team, you need to make it clear that you don't encourage that kind of culture and it won't get them any further personally or professionally. Similarly, in the world of hybrid work people are more likely to work from home when sick than take the day off, but if they're not able to do their best work you need to encourage them to take the time off to recover properly, which will lead to a faster return to full health.

You need to measure your team on output not how many hours they're seen to be working.

CHAPTER 11

MATERNITY, PATERNITY, FLEXIBLE WORKING AND OTHER FAMILY FRIENDLY RIGHTS

There is already plenty of information on the internet around these areas so my aim here is not to talk about the exact legalities of each of these employee rights but to make you aware that they exist and that as a Manager, you need to have a basic grasp of what your responsibilities are if a member of your team comes to you to say that they are:-

• Pregnant

• Adopting a child

• The partner of someone who is pregnant

• Experienced a miscarriage or stillbirth

• Changing genders

You can find plenty of information on the UK Government's website www.gov.uk on these subjects but also check your Company Handbook because many companies go beyond the statutory minimum. Typically you will see procedures for the following:-

- Maternity Leave

- Paternity Leave

- Adoption Leave

- Parental Leave

- Shared Parental Leave

- Parental Bereavement Leave

- Time off for Dependents

- Gender Reassignment

There is also a legal right for employees to request flexible working. This law now applies to all employees not just parents and carers, and is likely to change from 26 weeks service to qualify to day one of employment.

This isn't always just about someone wanting to come back part time after a period of maternity leave but could also be someone asking to temporarily or permanently change their contracted hours, work compressed hours, work at a different location etc.

You have a legal duty to consider each request seriously, and also some legally valid reasons to decline some requests. The key here is to be fair, and be consistent, but look at each case on its own merits.

If someone isn't satisfied with the outcome of their request they have a right to appeal once, and at the time of writing (December 2022), the law is likely to change so that they can make 2 requests in a 12 month period and you should look to resolve their request within 2 months.

CHAPTER 12
MANAGING IN A HYBRID WORLD

The art of managing people changed significantly during the pandemic of 2020 and beyond. When the majority of people were asked to work at home a lot of things suddenly changed. The 9-5 working where a manager was usually sitting somewhere nearby you was no longer a thing (unless you were doing work that couldn't be done at home), people were wearing less formal clothing, meetings went online via Zoom or Microsoft Teams, meetings got interrupted by the Amazon Delivery Driver, the child who was being home schooled, the inquisitive pet.

What interested me about this whole thing was that if Companies had taken a decision to implement home or hybrid working without a pandemic on it would have taken weeks if not months of meetings, policy writing, and presenting business cases to boards. In reality, we all had to make it happen overnight and generally from my experience, it worked.

When the COVID rules were relaxed, it was interesting to see what approach different Companies took. Some such as Goldman Sachs famously wanted everyone back in the office 5 days a week, whereas on the other extreme, Companies said "work from anywhere" and gave up their expensive leases on office premises in exchange for providing people with hubs and shared working spaces for collaboration where coming in for meetings was the exception and not the norm.

As things have progressed, many Companies that are able to are now operating a hybrid working system and trying to get the balance right between getting people in the office to collaborate, whilst giving people the flexibility they need.

Of course, home working works better for some people than others, and some types of work are better suited to hybrid working than others.

Rather than listing the advantages and disadvantages of hybrid working, I want to focus on how you go about leading a hybrid team as this way of working looks set to stay in many companies in one form or another.

Do	Don't
Make sure you check in on your team on a 1:1 and group basis. Find ways your team can still come together as one whether that's in person, over video or a mix of the two. Work on trust Support people who want to come into the office if they find it hard to work at home Look to get all your team together in person regularly if at all possible. (With a good reason)	Expect everyone there between 9-5 but focus on work output rather than the hours they're seen to be at their desk. (See "Presenteeism in Chapter 11) Try to enforce jollity unless you've cracked a great activity that works and actually engages people e.g. "fun Friday quiz" or similar.

Employees now want flexibility. They don't want to spend lots of money in a cost of living crisis on commuting to and from the office. Some do their best work first thing in the morning, others late at night. If employers fail to offer this, they are likely to lose out on good candidates who will want to work for employers who do offer this. However, I am still asked by many of my clients how they can get more people back in the office to build on their culture and encourage collaboration. For me, you need to give people a good reason to come in.

Although I prefer working at home, I always saw the value of coming into an office because you would have a random conversation with someone and learn something useful you wouldn't do if you were sitting in isolation at home. A mix to me is therefore good but in my view works best if the employer is nonprescriptive about how it will work. For example, instead of saying "everyone must come in for 3 days a week minimum" try saying instead "we trust you to make the right choices and come in when you need to for meetings, and we ask that you are present for XYZ but to use your judgement the rest of the time and come in when you need to, and work from home when that works best."

The latter view will show you trust your employees, are treating them like adults and trusting them to use their judgement and make sensible decisions. You'll find as a leader most people will relish this and can be trusted. For the minority that can't, you can tackle them on an individual case by case basis. (see earlier chapter about having difficult conversations)

CHAPTER 13

EQUITY (NOT EQUALITY), DIVERSITY AND INCLUSION

I'm writing a few words on this topic not just because it's the right thing to do in a book about how to manage people well but because it's something I am passionate about.

Let's start by talking about people in general – there has been a lot of talk about people feeling that they should be able to "bring their authentic selves to work". What does this mean in reality?

Whilst we may all think we have a work "persona" and we appear a certain way to our colleagues we are all still the same person and can't and shouldn't always hide who we really are to our colleagues. Easier said than done, right?

For me being able to do this is at the heart of a Company that truly believes in welcoming diversity and encouraging people from all backgrounds to be themselves. There's been a lot of talk on LinkedIn about whether tattoos should be visible at work. As someone who has four of them, it's not something I have an issue with and is something which is seen as more acceptable now than it once was. For people who still think it's an issue I would encourage them to consider why they have that feeling and if it really impacts on someone's ability to do their job well. If it does, then by all means raise it.

It also means if people are going through a tough time outside of work and they feel supported by their Manager they are less likely to go off sick, and may be able to get the help they need quicker if they feel they can talk to someone in confidence about what they're going through. This doesn't mean you have to fix their problem, but lend a friendly ear and signpost them in the right direction if you need to.

I also believe encouraging a diverse background helps you grow as a business as you can bring in different knowledge, experiences rather than everyone you hire being a carbon copy of yourself. But do this for the right reasons, not just because you want the "poster person" on your website.

Finally, it significantly reduces the chance of you getting a pesky discrimination claim from a disgruntled ex employee at a tribunal. Compensation for successful discrimination claims is uncapped. Even if you do get a claim if you are able to prove that you promote diversity and it's not just a box ticking paper exercise or a poster on the back of the toilet door, it will improve your chances of success.

What follows is an image that was originally put together by Craig Freohle, a Business Professor and has been adapted many times over the years but for me explains the difference between equality and fairness. Many people may argue that they don't like workplace diversity practices as they are perceived as giving unfair advantage to minority groups.

(Source: http://www.pugetsoundoff.org/blog/equality-versus-equity)

So for me this demonstrates a clear difference between Equality and Equity, and we should be striving for Equity.

CHAPTER 14

WELLBEING AND MENTAL HEALTH

It wouldn't be right to write a book without including a chapter about Wellbeing and Mental Health. As a People Leader, you have a legal duty of care towards your employees, and whilst an HR function can advise and support you in how to deal with employee absence and welfare issues, it's not my role to do that for you – the responsibility lies with you.

The pandemic and a series of lockdowns have highlighted to me that employee wellbeing is just as relevant now as it always has been, if not more so in that we have all seen employees struggle to deal with a disrupted world.

As a people leader, you need to get to know your team well so you notice behaviour patterns which appear to be out of character for that individual. This could be they are quieter than usual, more short tempered, appear distracted etc. The skill is to approach the employee in a sensitive and supportive way to try and find out what the root cause is. They may not know themselves, but here's where asking the right open questions can really help. (Hint : Ask questions where they can't just respond with a one word "yes" "no" answer). Offer support, and also know that you are not expected to be the expert, and may need to refer them to a specialist. Depending on who you work for this could be an Employee Advice Programme (EAP) Helpline, your locally appointed Mental Health First Aider, Occupational Health, or their GP. If you have an HR person (like me!) looking after your business they could also provide you with further information and places to go.

Don't assume that the situation will resolve itself, keep doing informal 1:1 check ins and offer support to any employees in your team who are struggling with their mental health. Offer practical solutions which are within your authority to do so to help them as a short-term measure. These could include, flexibility on when hours are worked, regular breaks from the workstation, a buddy or mentor etc. The fact you've been supportive and have intervened early will go a long way to stop the situation escalating.

But what about when employees "swing the lead"? Some will take advantage of a situation to be on sick leave that little bit longer than they need to be, or will get stressed out at the notion that you're asking them to do something they don't want to do. It happens. I get it. The best thing I can advise here is to tread carefully, and gather evidence to support your suspicions before acting on it. Usually as an HR professional, I will get a medical opinion from an Occupational Health provider which will usually flush out any exaggerations.

Here are 9 signs where you as a leader can have a positive impact on your team's mental health (Courtesy of "Hacking HR")

1. Employees Feel Safe – and can speak up without fear or retaliation

2. Employees Feel Appreciated – credit is given where it's due

3. You as leader know each person in your team, as a human not just an employee.

4. Your team can be their authentic selves. They don't have to hide who they really are.

5. You respect each member of your team, they respect each other, and you

6. You care about your team – you recognise their fears, vulnerabilities, strengths and talent.

7. They can be vulnerable around you

8. You support and challenge them – allowing continuous learning to take place.

9. You act with compassion and will help individuals to resolve their problems where you can.

CHAPTER 15

GIVING DIFFICULT FEEDBACK IN THE RIGHT WAY

Every manager dreads the difficult conversation with the employee who they feel will be difficult. I have coached many managers through these types of issues time and time again and here are my tips to how to do them well

- **Good Preparation** – It's not an exam! You are allowed to take your notes in with you. Have in mind what you want the outcome to be, and what you will be saying, and armed with the supporting evidence.

- **Location** – Try and choose the best place to have the chat. Face to face is best if you can do this, but if it has to be remotely, turn the video camera on and choose a quiet location where neither of you will be disturbed. Same with real life, turn your phone off and find a discreet location away from anyone who may overhear something or see the meeting taking place.

- **Tone** – Talk calmly, and slowly. If the employee starts to get upset you can give them a moment, but don't let the tears/tantrums stop you having the conversation. Pass the tissue box, but carry on.

- **Explain** – Go through with the employee the reason for why you want to meet with them, and give feedback as constructively as possible. Be clear and not vague. Don't forget to ask them for their thoughts on what you've said. Also whilst you may be referring to your notes, make sure that this is a genuine human conversation that involves good body language and eye contact. Don't just hide behind your laptop screen/note pad and read the conversation out like a script.

- **Outcome** – Be clear about what you want the outcome to be and ask what support they need from you to achieve this, and/or what support you will be giving them. Try and be as positive as possible.

- **Evidence** – Follow the conversation up with an e mail outlining expectations and agree follow up meeting if appropriate to make sure the progress has been made. If it has make sure you congratulate and thank the individual. If it hasn't consider taking further action you feel is necessary.

For more tips on this area I recommend the book "Fierce Conversations" by Susan Scott.

CHAPTER 16

RETAINING PEOPLE

I've already touched on having a good culture before but there are other things which are important. A Finances Online Survey conducted in September 2022 about reasons for why the millennial generation quit their job was:-

- Dissatisfaction with pay/financial rewards – 43%

- Not enough opportunities to advance – 35%

- They don't feel appreciated – 28%

- Lack of flexibility and poor work/life balance – 22%

- Boredom – 21%

- They don't like the workplace culture – 15%

A survey amongst my own network showed the top 5 reasons people (of all generations) may quit a role as being:-

- Poor Communication

- Burnout

- Undefined Roles

- Poor Flexibility

- Bad workplace culture/relationships

Recently the concept of the "silent resignation" has been discussed whereby managers don't want to go through a formal capability or disciplinary but deliberately make the workplace so bad some of their people vote with their feet and resign. This is not good practice, and here's where having robust timely feedback and becoming skilled at having difficult conversations really do come into their own.

So let's now look at the reasons people quit and see what you as a Manager can do about them:-

- **Financial Reward** – your company may have limited budgets for doing these, but it's always worth working with someone like me who can benchmark pay and benefits with other similar companies in your industry so you can see if you are underpaying. It's not always possible to counteroffer, and for some people no amount of extra money will make up for a toxic working environment. So it's important to get the other stuff right too

- **Career Progression** – Traditionally people used to think this involved being a "Manager" or "Team Leader" but actually there are so much more career paths that people can take. Not everyone wants to, or is suited to being a people manager (as I'm sure you may have seen from your own first hand experience of being an employee!). I've worked with Companies and helped them come up with alternative career paths, and been transparent about what these are so people can see that they can move up through the Company without looking elsewhere. For example, people could become Technical Experts, and Project Managers as well as or instead of a traditional People Manager. You also need to manage people's expectations that if they arrive on day 1 they won't be the MD within a year. Sometimes people need to move sideways as well as upwards to develop.

- **Appreciation** – Here is where one size most definitely doesn't fit all, and is a tricky one to get right. Sometimes a simple "thankyou" said in a timely and sincere way is all it takes to motivate someone. You're the manager and you've recognised them for something they have done well that maybe goes above and beyond what they'd normally do. Other ways you could reward them could be an instantaneous, low value gift voucher which is more timely than the traditional bonus. Not everyone is motivated by money so it's about finding things which are appropriate and fit in with the culture of your team.

- **Flexibility/Work Life Balance** Since the pandemic, the question most candidates ask at interview is about hybrid working and expectations around that. But it's not always around location, it could be hours too. Obviously certain types of roles have to be done with set hours and location or they wouldn't work, but if you're in an office or client facing role why not measure the team on output rather than being seen to be suited and booted at their desks between 9 and 5? Some people do their best work in the early hours of the morning at home, others are night owls and could work from a café. You should find the majority of people enjoy the trust that's placed in them to make these types of decisions and be treated like an adult and you would just need to deal with the small majority of people who abuse that trust. It also helps people with work life balance in terms of childcare/elder care/ being able to complete short domestic chores during the day rather than having to take leave for it. It also gives you a good reputation as an employer and could attract people to you who don't want to work for your competitors if they're more rigid.

- **Boredom** People generally want to be doing meaningful roles where they feel they are making a difference, have a purpose, and are doing work that is in line with their own personal ethics. Having worked in the Renewable Energy industry, I have met a lot of people who are passionate about the environment and that's why they chose to work for us, or they are scientists who like to discover new methods that can save the planet. When I've worked with Managed Service Providers/Tech Companies many of their employees enjoy problem solving and building good efficient solutions for their clients. Of course different things motivate different people and the skill of being a manager comes in getting to know your team and treating them as individuals and as consumers.

- I know there's no such thing as the perfect job out there and not every role can be totally thrilling all of the time, but you need to design your roles so people who want to feel like they're progressing, learning, and achieving things. But also be aware you have two very broad groups of people in the workplace. There are those that don't want to go anywhere, but just come in and do their job and go home again. And those that want to progress up the career ladder. There may not be the straight up ladder there was years ago as companies have flatter structures but people need to create their own and think about sideways moves as well as upwards. What I'm trying to say is that you need to work out which of your employees are which and still find ways to motivate them whilst they work for you.

CHAPTER 17

EXITING PEOPLE

Sometimes, despite your best efforts, it becomes all too clear that your employee and you need to part company.

Legally, you can dismiss an employee for several reasons:-

- Following a disciplinary or capability hearing where the offence is serious enough to do so and in line with your policy, or after a series of escalated warnings. These should be set out in your Company Handbook or stand alone Disciplinary/Capability policies.

- If someone is deemed medically incapable of performing their role and a medical professional has confirmed the same.

- A fixed term contract has come to an end

- Due to redundancy (where a role no longer exists)

- A statutory bar e.g. someone loses their driving licence in a driving role so unable to continue with it.

- Some other substantial reason

You will see I've not mentioned probation in there specifically. This is because probationary period doesn't really have a legal meaning, however many contracts of employment will state that typically the first three or six months will be subject to a probation/review period and that the notice period to dismiss will typically be shorter than the norm e.g. one week, or no notice at all.

As a first time line people leader, I would recommend that you never dismiss someone without seeking advice from your internal HR person or an external consultant like myself first as I help people avoid the pitfalls. Sure, some dismissals are more straight forward than others. If there is an existing dispute or it's "just not working out" subject to ensuring there are no potential tricky claims waiting in the background then sometimes it's better to have what's called a "protected conversation" or "Without Prejudice" Discussion meaning that employment usually ends by mutual agreement in exchange for a sum of money in addition to any other pay the employee would be contractually entitled to, such as notice or holiday. Again, something I help businesses to navigate successfully.

The best advice I can give people when it looks like someone's employment is likely to end in a termination is...

Tip 5: Evidence Everything!

There's no point having a conversation with someone if there's no audit trail/follow up e mail to prove it happened. So that way you can prove you are dismissing on the grounds of conduct or capability rather than discriminating against them for some reason or another. I liken it to a game of snakes and ladders – with no evidence you may need to start again gathering evidence. Place all issues in your regular catch ups and in writing.

Also it's important to

Tip 6: Exit with dignity.

Put yourself in the shoes of the employee. If they're about to be terminated due to poor performance they still need to find another job, where they're a better fit or the role is better matched to what skills they do have – always try and find a positive and manage the exit discreetly. Also work out what you're going to say to their now former colleagues without breaching confidentiality, and think about other risks e.g. stopping their IT access if they are likely to be disruptive.

Tip 7: Try to do it in under two years – 18 months or sooner is safer particularly if you have no HR support in your organisation.

The reason I say this is that employees gain more rights after two years' continuous service in the UK. They can make a claim for unfair, wrongful or constructive dismissal. All of which you will need to spend time and money in defending. Whereas for an employee, it's currently free to put in a Tribunal Claim using the ET1 form. Yes I know it's unfair, but that's the way it is.

Please be aware that employees can make some types of claims with under two years' service such as discrimination or victimisation due to making what's called a "protected disclosure" e.g. whistleblowing. However for the vast majority of cases lose the difficult people in well under two years.

The Silent Resignation

Recently there has been a lot of talk about "The Silent Resignation". It's referred to as when people are "phased out" of an organisation in the hope that if they're left out of key meetings, have responsibilities taken away from them or some other action that reduces their standing in the workplace they may take the hint and resign. Needless to say, I don't recommend this as a strategy. Not only does doing this increase the risk of you getting a successful constructive dismissal claim but it also makes you look like you can't have a difficult conversation. So please, just read the earlier advice about how to have a difficult conversation. Bite the bullet and do it. It may be painful at first but in the long run it will work out better if you're just honest with people. Also, please dismiss them for the right reason. Don't disguise poor performance as a "redundancy" situation because it isn't.

CHAPTER 18

TOP TEN MISTAKES MANAGERS MAKE

These are based on my own observations over a 20+ year career. Some of them I've had done to me, many I've seen myself, and many a time I've had to try and dig the relevant manager out of a difficult hole...

1] "It's my way or the highway"

For those managers who are in post because they like power and being in control, managing someone doesn't mean asserting your authority and thinking someone will bow down in revered honour will happen. It won't. They will get frustrated, they will lose any enthusiasm for the job and will leave, only to be replaced by someone else who will most likely do the same very quickly.

2] Giving a promotion to a poor performer

Otherwise known as moving a problem employee from position A to position B. I've seen several managers do this over the years – it's always failed. If someone isn't good at doing position A which is more junior. Chances are, promoting them to position B won't suddenly make them step up and become employee of the year. They will most likely struggle in terms of presenting the required behaviours and skills to do well. Therefore resulting in a protected conversation, a long drawn out capability procedure or worse still, doing nothing and annoying their other colleagues who will start to think that to get promoted they just have to not be very good and will stop making such an effort.

3] Not accepting the advice or expertise of others

A good leader will realise that they don't know it all, can't know it all, and will always need the advice of experts to help them. Whether that's at business owner/MD level when they want to grow a business or at first line/time manager level when they will be far from the finished article. Here's where having a good supportive network around you comes into its own. A good leader will welcome being constructively challenged and will take the advice of experts, these could take the form of:

- External Coach or Mentor

- A more experienced people manager

- A People expert/HR Consultant

- An internal subject matter expert

- An Accountant

- External network of peers etc.

It's how you grow as a person. I took lots of advice when I started my business, just as I did when I got promoted in my in house HR career. It helped me get better. The managers who don't do this can be spotted because they won't hire competent people around them as they don't like being challenged. They will instead hire "nodding dogs" who will always agree with them. This can be dangerous as without lots of different ideas a business/team cannot grow and it also leads to the Manager becoming stressed as every decision will have to be run past them at all times, meaning they don't have time to focus on what they should be doing.

4] Not being able to give up control

This leads neatly on from my last point. If you as a Manager can't give up control then you will get stressed because you can't focus on what you should be doing. Instead, look at your role and see which tasks if any could be done by someone else in your team. If you struggle to give these up ask yourself why. Is it that you don't feel in control? Or you don't trust members of your team to do things?

5] Not sharing knowledge

This also follows on from the last point. A good manager will look to share knowledge so their team grow and develop. Just do it, it will make your life easier in the long run. There's something wrong if there's a queue of people at your desk wanting you to make decisions or ask lots of questions on a regular basis, particularly if it relates to something they've done before and recently. When training people on how to do things, don't just explain what to do, explain the why as well so they understand how it fits into the bigger scheme of things. Ask them to make notes if they're not already and re-peat it back to you so you can check that they've understood properly.

6] Not changing with the times

"We've always done it that way" is not a good enough reason to keep on doing things the same. A former MD wisely said to me once if you don't move forward and stand still, you're ac-tually going backwards. Whilst your competitors are moving ahead. Keep developing yourself, keep learning new ideas.

But know which ones to implement and which ones may just be passing fads and which ones may not be right for your team/department.

7] Not supporting their team members when they're right

As a Manager you need to be seen to stand by the decisions your team have made wherever possible, particularly if they're the right ones. If they're the wrong ones then address it privately with the individual(s) concerned but don't criticise them in front of other people.

8] Not promoting the right culture

I've already talked about this in Chapter 3 – Culture Club, but I'd make the point again here that every manager should promote the right culture, and promote the company culture which should, be in line with their own personal values about the way they like to do things.

9] Not tackling issues promptly that arise within the team

I remember having a manager 20 years ago I sat a few feet away from on a daily basis, but decided to wait until my annual appraisal before bringing up any areas of concern, rather than just talking to me about them informally as and when so I had the opportunity to correct them. Hopefully if your organisation is progressive enough, the annual review has already been consigned to the dustbin where I think it belongs. However if it hasn't – don't be that manager that uses a formal process to hide behind taking any action. Instead, have regular check ins, little and often with your team, raise issues as they happen and give praise where it's due too.

10] Getting too emotive/emotionally close to your team. They aren't your family.

Many organisations I know try and say "we're like one big family" which I really dislike! Whilst these comments are often well intentioned I find it's not helpful to think of your colleagues and your direct reports in this way. Other than divorcing a partner, do you really fire members of your family, or expect them to be devoted to you unconditionally for a set number of hours per week? I'm also sure that you probably don't speak to your nearest and dearest in the same way that you speak to your work colleagues.

As a Manager, it's important that you don't appear too distant from your team, giving the perception that you consider yourself to be better than them or emotionally detached. As I've said before, get to know them, the names of their partners/kids/pets/hobbies etc and engage with them as you're more likely to get buy in and loyalty back. You could even go and have a drink with them too if you are comfortable doing that and it's appropriate for your workplace and the culture.

But that said, you still need to keep a bit of distance as someone can't always be your mate if you need to have a difficult conversation with them the following week, or go through a formal process with them. Learn to find that right balance, and know where the line is that you don't want to cross.

CASE STUDY

This story happened to a former colleague of mine who was happy for me to share their experiences in this book.

I reported into a newly promoted manager who wanted to be everyone's mate and would tell you what you wanted to hear in order to avoid confrontation at all costs. I remember going to this particular individual as I'd spent the night before crying because a member of our team had been real-

ly unkind to me for a period of time. This particular person had made comments about my marriage not lasting, they were loud and rude and would e mail other people across the desks and laugh out loud. This was workplace bullying. It took a lot of courage for me to speak to my line manager and when I did their exact words were "I think the problem is that they are jealous because they're fat and you're not!"

I couldn't believe my manager was excusing someone's bullying behaviour because of their weight. They offered me no solution or support and I walked away wishing that I was perhaps fat so I could avoid the daily insults. This particular manager worked her way around the organisation telling people what they wanted to hear rather than what was effective for the organisation.

I've since had great bosses and bad ones too but a lot of the time it comes down to a good manager that listens, is professional, fair and who has realistic expectations.

Key learnings here:-

Managers have to sometimes put themselves in uncomfortable positions by addressing situations rather than trying to keep everyone happy.

CHAPTER 19

THE FUTURE OF WORK

Whether we like it or not, the world of work will be continuing to change over the next few decades. We all noticed a big shift during the 2020 pandemic when it suddenly became possible for many roles to work from home instead of commuting to a place of work on a daily basis, which appealed to many, and is now one of the key questions asked about a role when people apply. This would have not been possible before that, other than permission to work from home on very ad hoc occasions for many organisations.

There have been some famous critics of hybrid working, such as Lord Sugar and Goldman Sachs Bank. But like it or not, hybrid working looks set to stay in one form or another.

However I don't see the world of work stopping there. I've read many reports that say that things will continue to evolve and by the year 2030 artificial intelligence (AI) will have found a way of replacing a lot of roles which currently exist across many industries and sectors with more automation replacing the need for a person to carry out a particular activity. Chat GBT is already starting to make an impact.

A positive for people is that life may be more about pleasure and time off and less about living to work, more about working to live – but the downside could mean that there are fewer jobs around, or that roles will change and need a new skills set for people to be able to carry them out.

I personally believe the success of this lies within the education system changing to prepare the students of today for the challenges of the world of work tomorrow as well as teaching valuable life skills such as how to manage a budget, build key relationships etc. Sadly, the reality of what is taught in schools doesn't always equip people for the future in the way that it should.

So what can you as a People Leader be thinking about now?

Firstly, don't form a protective bubble around your team and resist all change. Have a think about future proofing your team, look at the work you do, what you may need to do in the future in line with your Company's overall vision and strategy and think about what tasks might be automated and how, and what types of roles you may need now and in the future, and train your staff up so they're ready to take them on.

Also think about how you can automate more menial tasks now, not only does this save on wages but it means the people in your team can hopefully take on more challenging and enjoyable tasks than doing basics.

Hopefully it will also show your own managers/board that you are thinking about the future and keen to be part of it, and have lots of good ideas to make the company future proof.

You don't want to end up as the next Kodak or Blockbuster...

CHAPTER 20

PEOPLE STRATEGY AND MANAGING CHANGE

A lot of what we've covered so far is the stuff I wish I'd known when I started out as a line manager some 20 years ago, along with what other line managers have told me they wished they had known when they started out.

Very few managers think about their actual people strategy. This goes beyond turning up to work each day and checking your team are OK and giving them operational advice and guidance when they ask for it, or you sense they need it. Whilst a People strategy is often put together by a Board, a Managing Director/CEO or an HR person, it's important that you know what it is and think about how it can apply to your team.

It shouldn't be seen as a mystical bit of navel gazing, or be a really long document that no one will ever read and will go out of date instantly, but in short, a People strategy should be…

A plan outlining the steps to get from where you are now (A) to where you want to be (B)

As I mentioned earlier in this book, you need to be thinking about what your team could look like in the future as a result of changes to Technology, the Industry you're in, or the Company's future plans for expansion or slimming down. From there, you work out what skills/processes you have now and think about what you need in the future.

Much simpler than lots of competency matrixes!

I've mentioned change a lot in this book already. There are whole books out there on the subject of change management. So my aim here is to just give an overview of the subject by saying –

The key point of successfully managing any kind of change is to get your people to buy into the change and come on that journey with you.

People will make their decisions usually based on emotion rather than logic. So rather than giving your team stats about how a change you're proposing will benefit the Company, tell them a story instead about how it will make their working lives better, paint a picture for what the future could look like and how they could get involved.

CHAPTER 21
NEXT STEPS

If you've found this book helpful but would like further remote or in person support from me, in addition to the advice in this book I offer several packages which will help you.

If you're an individual newly promoted people leader I can work with you on a 1:1 basis to find out more about you, your team and give you strategies to help you make the successful transition from colleague to people leader. Please contact me using the details below for a free no obligation chat where we will see if we're a good fit for each other.

As a thank you for buying this book, if you use the code LEADERSHIP, you will get a 20% discount on any courses that are booked within 3 months of you buying this book (show me proof of purchase)

For more information go to www.surebettshr.com/leadershipcoaching

Business Owners

Does any of this apply to you?

- You google your HR queries

- You get your PA/Accountant to look after the people function although it's not their area of expertise.

- You've had to spend a lot of time dealing with staff issues as your manager's don't know what they're doing and it's stopping you focussing on what you want to do – growing your business and making a profit.

Here's where I can also help you. Either on a project or an ongoing basis depending on your needs to help you solve the following problems you may be experiencing in your business.

- High Staff Turnover

- Problems hiring the right people

- Incorrect employment documentation that's not in line with UK Law

- Not knowing how your pay and benefits packages compare to your competition.

- Helping line managers make the right decisions in relation to their people

- Having someone on hand at a fraction of the cost of an in house Director of People and Culture to bounce ideas off and help you plan your people strategy

- Helping you to give your employees a great experience so they don't ever want to leave!

I offer a "Done for you" HR service – you can subscribe to me from as little as £249 per month to just have me available for ongoing advice when you need it. You can add projects to this and spread the cost over the subscription period too, which include:-

- Audit Requirements – getting Contracts, and people friendly policies in place/reviewing current practices.

- Setting up an HR function for new businesses to make sure the employee experience runs smoothly.

- Creating modern job descriptions and evaluating your pay and benefits package.

- Helping you work out your business mission, values and culture and translate this into a people plan which will reduce turnover and increase productivity.

- Running individual and group coaching sessions (minimum 3 months) for newly promoted People Managers to help them hit the ground running. This can be done on an individual 1:1 basis or group coaching with teams in a specific organisation. I also collaborate with a Mindset Coach where we work together on improving employee wellbeing at work whilst coaching individuals on how to be great people leaders. These sessions have lots of practical tips as well as focussing on each individual and the team(s) they lead.

There's a variety of options available and courses can be done in person, or online.

Please get in touch with me via https://calendly.com/doug-betts for a free no obligation chat.

If you'd like to download my FREE employment law checklist go to https://www.surebettshr.com/employment-law-checklist

If you're not looking to work with me yet but would like some free hints/tips from me and to receive my monthly newsletter join my mailing list at https://www.surebettshr.com/contact and type "Newsletter" in the subject line.

Follow me on Social Media via : https://linktr.ee/dougbetts. I also post regular YouTube videos on a variety of relevant HR/Manager topics.

Or, just scan this QR Code to go straight to my LInktree page:-

Finally, thankyou for reading my book, I hope you have found it useful and it helps you develop your skills as a great people leader.

ABOUT THE AUTHOR

Doug was born and grew up in Ipswich, Suffolk.

Doug's HR career started in 2001 in the public sector and in the past 20+ years he's undertaken a wide range of HR roles across the public, private and not-for-profit sectors, in both in house up to Director level as well as consultancy roles. His clients have ranged from businesses owned by MP's to establishments connected with the Royal Family.

Doug has always been very driven determined to make a career for himself, but realised he gets the the greatest satisfaction from helping others. In this case, it's businesses who don't know how to manage people correctly or run into legal difficulties around people leadership. Doug gets great satisfaction from working with clients and seeing his ideas make a positive difference to numerous workplaces.

Away from HR, Doug enjoys travelling, is a Grade 8 pianist (but prefers playing indie/pop/rock to classical) and runs marathons and half marathons. He also enjoys a good craft beer and spending time with friends.

He's not done yet and is looking to continue to grow his consultancy "Sure Betts HR Solutions" as well as his collaboration "Better People Connections".

Printed in Great Britain
by Amazon

54679261R00066